Updates on Software Usability

Edited by Laura M. Castro

Published in London, United Kingdom

Updates on Software Usability
http://dx.doi.org/10.5772/intechopen.102281
Edited by Laura M. Castro

Contributors
Josef Pavlíček, Petra Pavlíčková, Robert Strohmaier, Gerhard Sprung, Sandra Schadenbauer, Alexander Kurt Nischelwitzer, Steve McKeever, Luiza Fabisiak, Barbara Jagielska, Laura M. Castro

First published in London, United Kingdom, 2023 by IntechOpen
IntechOpen is the global imprint of INTECHOPEN LIMITED, registered in England and Wales, registration number: 11086078, 5 Princes Gate Court, London, SW7 2QJ, United Kingdom

British Library Cataloguing-in-Publication Data
A catalogue record for this book is available from the British Library

Additional hard and PDF copies can be obtained from orders@intechopen.com

Updates on Software Usability
Edited by Laura M. Castro
p. cm.
Print ISBN 978-1-80356-635-1
Online ISBN 978-1-80356-636-8
eBook (PDF) ISBN 978-1-80356-637-5

Meet the editor

Dr. Laura M. Castro is a professor at the University of A Coruña, Spain, where she has been lecturing for more than fifteen years. Apart from being a coordinator of several undergraduate courses on software architecture and software testing, she is currently the president of the Institutional Chair for Open Science Promotion through Software (CICAS). Her most recent research interests focus on the automatic validation of distributed systems. She has supervised three Ph.D. theses and acted as principal investigator for several European projects. She is also actively involved in dissemination activities, in particular the visibility of women in STEM, as a member of the Association for Computing Machinery's Council on Women in Computing (ACM-W) Europe.

Contents

Preface

This book is an update to the book *Software Usability*, which was published only a couple of years ago. Why is it that we need an update so soon? The good news is that it is not a matter of the knowledge, techniques, or tools becoming obsolete, which is something that does sometimes happen in the tech world. Rather, it is a sign that the reflections, efforts, and work in this area are still expanding. This is good news as society adopts more and more software for both professional and personal uses.

In this updated volume, we have broadened the perspectives from which software usability is considered. That is, the book considers developers and technology makers as *users* of software tools themselves. Even if very knowledgeable, self-confident, and autonomous learners, developers are some of the most intensive software users there are! Still, a significant part of this book's content focuses on the process of making software *for the people*.

This volume includes a collection of high-quality contributions to software usability for developers and non-developers alike. While presenting novel research and experiences, the book is also suited for the general reader. It is designed to disseminate new ideas, making them *accessible* to people who might not be software *makers* but who are undoubtedly software *users*.

Dr. Laura M. Castro
Department of Computer Science and Information Technologies,
University of A Coruña,
A Coruña, Spain

Section 1

Preliminaries

Chapter 1

Introductory Chapter: Why Usability Matters

Laura M. Castro

1. Introduction

1.1 Usability and software development

Despite what it may seem at times in the context of software development nowadays, *usability* is a rather old term. It was first defined in 1998 by the International Standards Organization as part of ISO 9241-11: 1998. At the time, *usability* was defined as "*the degree to which a software can be used by specified consumers to achieve quantified objectives with effectiveness, efficiency, and satisfaction in a quantified context of use*" [1].

It took two decades to review this document, two decades in which software and people interact with software, have changed enormously, and continues to change [2]. The ISO 9241-11:1998 is now superseded by ISO 9241-11:2018 [3], but the definition of *usability* has changed very little: "*extent to which a system, product or service can be used by specified users to achieve specified goals with effectiveness, efficiency and satisfaction in a specified context of use.*" So, it would seem that, even if we have moved from orange/green monochrome monitors attached to very limited hardware in large companies' offices to ubiquitous high-resolution pocket-fitting devices, the main concerns should still be three: effectiveness, efficiency, and satisfaction.

The paradox about software is that applications and systems have become tools for other disciplines, and thus are being used to determine how they approach usability. In other words, as architects, engineers, and even fashion designers, use 3D models, AR, and VR, to test their creations, software is allowing them to improve user experience in fields from architecture [4] to food packaging [5]. The number of publications in these fields that have to do with usability shows a similar trend, same as the general interest in usability, according to people's online searches (see **Figure 1** and **Table 1**).

Thus, we could argue that the usability of software products is somewhat a key to usability in many (and increasing) aspects of our daily lives.

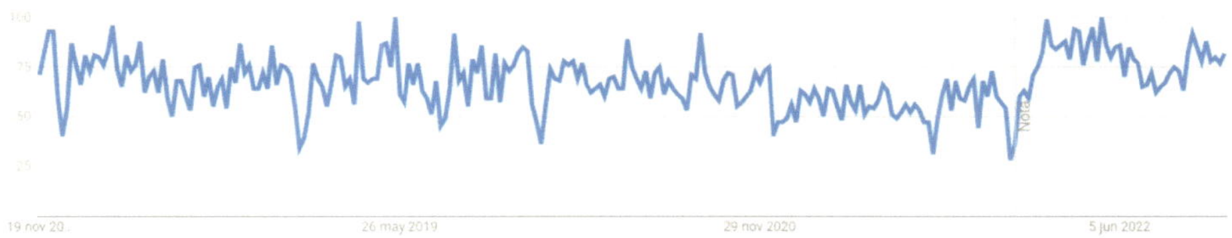

Figure 1.
Global searches related to "usability" (source: Google Trends).

	Computer Science	Architecture[1]	Engineering	Food[2]
2022[3]	825	25	452	25
2021	1203	45	605	17
2020	1268	24	575	14
2019	1398	29	725	13
2018	1124	25	509	14
2017	1096	36	474	15

[1]*Taken as part of the "Arts and Humanities" category in SCOPUS.*
[2]*Taken as part of the "Agricultural and Biological Sciences" category in SCOPUS.*
[3]*We include 2022, even if it is still ongoing at the time of writing this chapter.*

Table 1.
Number of scientific papers related to usability (data source: SCOPUS).

Last but not least, although almost all the time *usability* is about the user, software developers are heavy users of software themselves, specifically software development tools and applications. However, even if "programmers are users too" [6], there is comparatively far less research in their direction.

2. The side-effects of usability

The ill effects of bad usability depend highly on the context and purpose for which software is used. Of course, there is no comparison between angry users that turns to other social networks or music streaming platforms, and the health-threatening consequences of usability failures [7, 8]. However, bad software usability might affect, as stated in the previous section, any field that uses software as a tool, even archaeology [9].

While rating the severity of usability failures [10] is a sensible *afterward* approach to what was not detected before, same as in software testing, the efforts that pay off the most are those aimed to prevent usability failures from happening in the first place [11].

Something that cannot possibly be quantified is the harm done to the whole software development industry as a whole, and to the regard in which society holds technology and technology makers, when usability issues slip through to the final users, the regular citizens [12].

3. Conclusions and challenges ahead

Quoting Melvin Kranzberg, "Technology is not positive, nor negative, nor neutral" [13]. A biased development team, organization, and societal context... will most likely produce biased software. No team produces unusable software on purpose, but rather fails to understand what *usability* means to their users, in terms of its three key components: effectiveness, efficiency, and satisfaction.

Unsuited (biased and unusable) technology is not only a cause for unhappy people, but it may also lead to failed projects and economic losses. From a higher-level perspective, it may even perpetuate stereotypes and hinder the empowerment of minorities and underrepresented groups. Ultimately, the unsuitability of technology delays innovation and progress.

So far, the most effective ways of fighting biases in technology that we know are: (a) being aware of said biases, in all their shapes and forms, and (b) strive to have as much diverse development teams and organizations. From the perspective of usability, we can work toward the construction of more inclusive, thoughtful ways of interacting with software by carefully analyzing the individuals and societal non-functional requirements, and being aware of the influence of cultural and geographical differences in the three key pillars: effectiveness, efficiency, and satisfaction.

The future ahead comes with unprecedented challenges: the myth of the digital natives was debunked [14, 15], but will the digital divide with senior citizens [16] really fade away as generations of developers age themselves? Or will new technologies appear once again, and will the software development industry stumble on the same ineffective, inefficient, and dissatisfactory stone?

Author details

Laura M. Castro
Universidade da Coruña, A Coruña, Spain

*Address all correspondence to: lcastro@udc.es

References

[1] ISO 9241-11:1998 Ergonomic requirements for office work with visual display terminals (VDTs)—Part 11: Guidance on usability [Internet]. 1998. Available from: https://www.iso.org/standard/16883.html

[2] Eischen K. The Social Impact of Informational Production: Software Development as an Informational Practice. UC Santa Cruz: Center for Global, International and Regional Studies. 2002. Available from: https://escholarship.org/uc/item/9rp0c3w4

[3] ISO 9241-11:2018 Ergonomics of human-system interaction — Part 11: Usability: Definitions and concepts [Internet]. 2018. Available from: https://www.iso.org/standard/63500.html

[4] Bittencourt MC, do Valle Pereira D, Lúcia V, Júnior WP. The usability of architectural spaces: Objective and subjective qualities of built environment as multidisciplinary construction. Procedia Manufacturing. 2015;**3**:6429-6436. DOI: 10.1016/j.promfg.2015.07.919

[5] Goswami B. The Role of Food Packaging. Chapter of the Book: Global Challenges and Innovation in Science and Management. Delhi: KAAV Publications; 2019

[6] Myers BA, Ko AJ, LaToza TD, Yoon YS. Programmers are users too: Human-centered methods for improving programming tools. In Computer. 2016;**49**(7):44-52. DOI: 10.1109/MC.2016.200

[7] Alnosayan N, Chatterjee S, Alluhaidan A, Lee E, Feenstra LH. Design and usability of a heart failure mHealth system: A pilot study. JMIR Human Factors. 2017;**4**(1). DOI: 10.2196/humanfactors.6481

[8] Johnson ME, Willey N. Usability failures and healthcare data Hemorrhages. IEEE Security & Privacy. 2011;**9**(2):35-42. DOI: 10.1109/MSP.2010.196

[9] Traviglia A. Archaeological usability of hyperspectral images: Successes and failures of image processing techniques. BAR International Series. 2006;**1568**:123-130

[10] Sauro J. Rating the Severity of Usability Problems [Internet]. 2013. Available from: https://measuringu.com/rating-severity

[11] Horgan JR, Mathur AP. Software testing and reliability. In: Lyu MR, editor. The Handbook of Software Reliability Engineering. New York: McGraw-Hill; 1996. pp. 531-565

[12] Lauesen S. IT project failures, causes and cures. IEEE Access. 2020;**8**:72059-72067. DOI: 10.1109/ACCESS.2020.2986545

[13] Kranzberg M. Technology and History: "Kranzberg's Laws". Technology and Culture. 1986;**27**(3):544-560. DOI: 10.2307/3105385

[14] Bennett S, Maton KA, Kervin L. The 'digital Natives' Debate: A Critical Review of the Evidence. 2008. Available from: https://ro.uow.edu.au/edupapers/1149

[15] The digital native is a myth. Nature. 2017;**547**(380). DOI: 10.1038/547380a

[16] van Dijk JAGM. Digital divide research, achievements and shortcomings. Poetics. 2006;**34**(4-5):221-235. DOI: 10.1016/j.poetic.2006.05.004

Section 2

Designing for Usability

Chapter 2

Designing "Landing Page" for Websites Based on the User Experience: Review, Analysis, and Interpretation

Luiza Fabisiak and Barbara Jagielska

Abstract

The primary web design method is user experience-based "landing page" web design. It enables you to expand the reach of a particular company, institution, or application. It aims to present the most relevant information on the owner's website. A simple approach, such as split A/B testing, can provide reliable data because it includes an appropriate set of alternatives. This article provides an overview, analysis, and interpretation of the results obtained. It presents good and bad practices of existing landing pages. The approach showed optimal solutions in aggregate, segmented, and individual site users.

Keywords: UX, user experience, landing page, Adobe creative suit, website, webpage, A/B tests, CTA, dark patterns

1. Introduction

Nowadays, when creating a brand, or a product, one should take proper care of its advertising and kind of image. You need to clearly define the vision - what the product will be associated with, whether it is good enough and whether there will be demand for it. In the online world, achieving such a goal is much simpler than in the past - you can set up a website to present your offer. However, there are challenges involved - competition is even more significant than ever. You need to be original and, at the same time, follow current trends and outlined guidelines. It is necessary to exist and prove that life with our product will turn out to be simpler, more functional, and easier to use. A landing page was created to understand our clients and know their needs to encourage them to buy or make a specific profit. This page contains all critical information about the potential customer while offering relevant product information. Creating a catchy landing page requires a wealth of knowledge in the fields of user experience, web architecture, marketing, and analysis of the data collected by the owner. This study aims to analyze and interpret the perception of website landing page prototypes and their templates created with Adobe software by users of different age groups based on user experience.

2. Overview of methodologies and techniques for creating a landing page based on user experience

A landing page, otherwise known as a landing page, allows you to expand the reach of a particular company, institution, or application. Its purpose is to present the most relevant information on the owner's website. Users are redirected to a landing page when they click on a link, advertisement, newsletter, or even online shopping. Thus, it is a page to which one is redirected - usually from other portals. However, one can also be redirected within a given system, site, or application - for example, to another tab, such as purchasing or signing up for a mailing list. Profit is the key word - a landing page is supposed to provide profit - in the form of financial, more observers, more demand for a particular product, or simply visitors to the site [1].

A landing page is directly related to concepts such as Google Ads, Google Analytics, or at least the user experience itself - its task is to gather information from users - or, more specifically, to motivate them to perform the actions on the page. For example, registering on a website, signing up for a newsletter, or purchasing a specific product or service [2]. The task of a landing page is to attract as many users as possible to act. For this reason, tools such as Google Ads and Google Analytics are needed to control, and analyze users' data, track their movements inside the site and advertise to get them to the landing page. Google Ads and Google Analytics are undoubtedly some of the more critical user experience tools - with them, you can improve the content found on portals or web vortals.

A landing page has several essential elements that must be present on it. Among the most critical components of a properly executed landing page are:

- Clarity - little scrolling on the page, focus on the primary purpose,
- Simplicity - the least amount of text and elements is advisable,
- Visual appeal - corresponding to the basics of color scheme and typography on websites,
- Catchy and short CTA (call-to-action), i.e., a call to action - for example, "Create an account" instead of "Create an account on our site today."

Like any website, a landing page should also be fast, mobile-friendly, and secure [3]. The landing page can be divided into:

- Sales Landing Page - for selling goods, services,
- Lead Generation - for collecting customer data,
- Coming Soon - to inform about the event that will happen/product that will be on sale,
- Click Through - to direct to another page.

A landing page is an excellent tool for market research, competition, and analysis [4].

2.1 Methodologies for creating and elements of UX-oriented landing pages

Google Ads and Google Analytics play a significant role in landing page design. Thanks to them, the portal owner, or UX designer, can create the ideal marketing persona or document for the prospects who use a given site. Thanks to these tools, we can find out who is interested in the content appearing on a page. We can find out, for example - where the person is from, their age, education, or employment. Of course, these are not the only supporting tools. Based on this information, an experienced UX designer can determine a prospect's motivations and concerns. What influences their decisions, what their typical day looks like, or what goal they want to achieve by using the service are additional information that can infer from this information [5].

2.1.1 CTA, or call to action

A vital landing page element is the so-called CTA button or calls to action button. It is usually located in a prominent place in the very center of the site. It should stand out from other elements. This button is supposed to convey clear and precise information - what will happen when the user clicks on it? The information should be short, concise, striking, and simple in its message.

2.1.2 Graphic interface and typography of the landing page

The essence of most websites, including landing pages, is their design. The characteristic elements of a landing page, for example, are the CTA mentioned in Section 2.1.1. However, a call to action is not the only element of a landing page.

Limited text is a must. Fineness and detail are by no means advisable when designing such a page. What matters is the quick transmission of the essential information. Usually, it is the first seconds of the reception of a given site that determines the attraction of the viewer's attention [6].

The text is naturally connected with the font, size, type, or placement. Typography is an essential aspect of a landing page. The placement of typography depends mainly on the background and the page's image. In addition, it is a good idea to vary the size of fonts for headings and buttons versus the page content itself. Line spacing is also crucial, as well as line width - the maximum width is about 70 characters, corresponding to the width of A4-sized text [7]. The text must also contrast well so that it is easy to read. At most, the site should have two fonts - for example, headlines and text. It is also good practice to choose "standard" fonts - ones that the user has probably seen before (e.g., Helvetica or Arial).

Testimonials or customer logos are an exciting element that may or may not appear on our landing page. Testimonials are short videos usually containing a customer's opinion about our product. In it, he expresses his experience with it. They help and encourage a potential future observer of our site to make a purchase. Logos of known or existing customers, on the other hand, will inspire confidence that our product is made reliably and that someone is already using it. Any certificates, awards, or prizes in competitions can also be an additional asset [8]. Another confidence-inspiring element can be to show your contact information, such as your phone number, email, or business address.

2.1.3 Dark patterns

Dark patterns are deliberate practices that various companies or institutions use to achieve certain benefits, usually marketing or financial [9]. While these practices are legally legal, they are hardly ethical solutions. Therefore, it is quite a risky user experience practice.

These are online behaviors designed to manipulate viewers into doing something they **do not** necessarily want to do, such as joining an unsolicited newsletter to access a particular website or read an article.

Dark patterns can include, for example, bait and switch, forced disclosure, roach motel, forced continuity, friend spam, misdirection, sneak into the basket, confirm shaming, trick questions, privacy Zuckering, triggering fear, and disguised advertisements [10]. In **Figure 1**, you can see a typical example of a dark bait and switch pattern. This is one of the more commonly used dark patterns. It deceives the viewer by displaying several links, buttons, or redirection options on a given area of the website. In this situation, the user is often misled and does not necessarily click on the link they wanted. Clicking on another can, for example, download an unwanted program or, as in the example below, update your computer system.

Dark patterning is very controversial among the design community or web architects. Undoubtedly, they can bring a lot of benefits to a given site. However, it can also harm it. Viewers can easily be discouraged by such practices and thus abandon visiting a particular site. Equally, many corporations use them for their profits, but many abandon them for the sake of ethics and certain unwritten norms [12].

2.2 Examples of good and bad practices in landing page design

A landing page is also a website, so creating it should be guided by existing design principles. The fundamental rules are user experience, **esthetics**, Gestalt principles, limited color palette, fit for mobile devices, security, and typography [13]. However, the landing page has a couple of elements that need special attention - these are what distinguish it from other tabs on a given website.

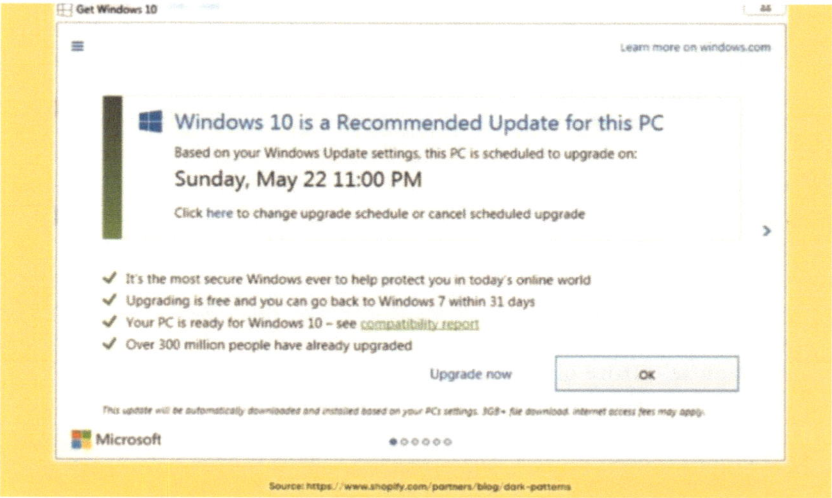

Figure 1.
Example of recipient deception, bait, and switch [11].

2.2.1 Good practices

One of the correct practices is a *header that precisely indicates the value* - the button should be above the fold. This element should be the most visible element on the page.

Another important aspect is the **form** - how long it should be and whether it collects only the most relevant user information. For example - an irrelevant piece of information will be the user's ownership of animals if you have a stock market website. From the perspective of meeting a business objective, you need to make sure that it is of sufficient length and that it does not also collect sensitive data from the recipient. Many users may become discouraged and not visit the site in question. The collection of sensitive data must be justified and explained [14].

Simple design is undoubtedly a trend in recent years in the design of all kinds of web pages. However, designing a landing page also has another use - it focuses only on its most crucial element - conversion, i.e., acquiring contact and then profit (e.g., selling a product, joining a mailing list). Distracting the viewer with an overly creative and colorful page is not advisable [15].

From a marketing perspective, page load time is essential for a landing page. According to a Google study, only 15% of respondents met the goal of loading a page in no more than 5 seconds [16]. This is an essential factor as it affects the final audience.

Another good practice in landing page design is a **graphic** or **video** showcasing our site's product. This is a very modern trend that can become a factor in attracting even more watchers. Interest in the product is one aspect, but if it is shown in an attractive, interesting, creative way - it will attract more takers. Recently, a very commonly used scheme is videos that stretch across the entire screen resolution, but you must remember to optimize these videos. They can slow down a given page a lot [**14**]. Often an adequately selected graphic is called a "hero shot." If the photo, the graphic, supports the message, the intention of the page, and fits the offer - it means that it was chosen correctly [**8**].

Critical practice is **customer feedback** - very often, we check the observations and ratings of others on a product. Their insights can warn against a potentially unsuccessful purchase or encourage us to make a good investment. It's worth posting them somewhere in the middle or end of our landing page - an essential and good practice but not the most important one from a marketing perspective [17].

Concise and understandable is the key to a well-executed landing page. The page should convey as little content as possible, which at the same time will be overflowing with helpful information. It is worth operating with the so-called "language of benefits" - what the user will gain by owning the product and what conveniences accompany the purchase. The creation of a personal document allowed the creation of more targeted content by understanding consumer needs [**18**].

2.2.2 Malpractices

Placing navigation at the top of our website can discourage the user - he will quickly change our site to another one. Any buttons should be in the center of our subpage. The lack of user interaction makes our landing page just an ordinary website. Conversion is a critical element of a landing page and should not forget - it is not only an unfair practice but also considerable negligence.

Complicated design only distracts the potential user. The recipient will most often abandon the use of our site without reading the information on it.

If the page takes **too long to load**, it will easily discourage a prospective buyer from doing anything. If the page does not load quickly, the recipient may assume that the services offered by the owner will not be of very high quality either, or perhaps will not reach him. It is, therefore, worth optimizing this page.

A **mismatched ad** on the landing page will confuse any viewer. The user needs to know that they have come to the right place. Hence the ad must contain the same message. Raising doubts in observers is not advisable [17].

3. Landing page prototypes

They made four pairs of prototype landing pages to test users' general knowledge of web design and user experience. In each of the five pairs of landing page prototypes, you can see the differences between versions A and B. For simplicity, version A is at the top of a given pair - version B at the bottom. The prototypes were made so that in some of the pairs, the differences were already apparent when first looking at them. In others, the differences are only apparent on closer inspection. The prototypes presented were also arranged the same way in the survey - as the first set varies the most. Thanks to this procedure, it was also possible to differentiate the approach of the respondents - whether they focused their attention on the general, the whole, or the details of the pairs of prototypes. A pair of prototypes that differed little would define the respondents' approach to focusing only on the details. The landing page prototypes differed in typography, color scheme, overall visual aspect, as well as on the quality of the selected images, and a modern approach in design such as neomorphism, in which 2D or 3D elements take on a background color giving the impression of being very uniform, even merged.

During the creation of the prototypes, followed both good and bad design practices to determine whether the average web user can perceive these differences and has a basic knowledge of web design, in this case, landing pages.

The prototype presented is "Veggie's," whose differences are immediately apparent - the A version has less opacity and has only one typographic font. The elements do not generally contrast as well as in the B version. Version B additionally uses two font types - for the informational text and a standard font for the logo and the button with the CTA. In addition, the A version logo washes out the background color is taken from the darkest point of the background photo, whereas in the B version, the white color contrasts with the photo. It enhances the logo, and it is more readable.

Therefore, version B is the correct version regarding user experience and design principles (**Figure 2**).

The next pair of prototypes show the hotel accommodation search service "hotelandresortspa.eu". The main difference in this pair is the color scheme of the two versions - the first is dominated by purple-blue, while the second is pink. In both versions, they are **esthetically** pleasing and match the background photo. According to design rules, however, the color scheme should relate to the background photo - so in theory, users should lean towards version A (**Figure 3**).

However, many users subconsciously choose solutions that feature contrast, characteristic of design trends in the past. Thus, it can conclude that both are done correctly in this pair of prototypes, but one is more in line with today's standards. However, it is likely that both, with a larger sample of users, would be considered correct - depending on the user's age, i.e., the likely seniority of Internet use and their preference for site design (**Figure 4**).

The final prototype is a prototype in which current web design principles create versions A and version B. Version B uses neomorphic elements - elements that merge colorfully with the background elements modeled on 3D graphics (**Figure 5**).

Figure 2.
First pair of prototypes.

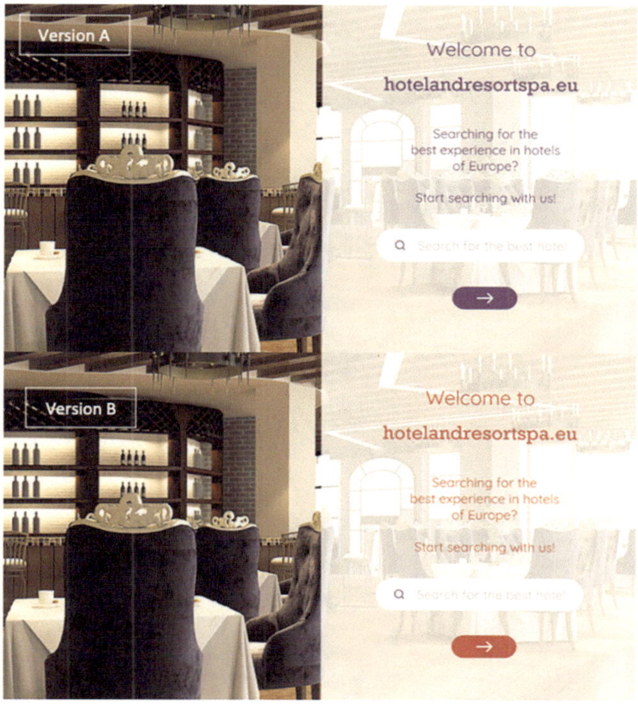

Figure 3.
Second pair of prototypes.

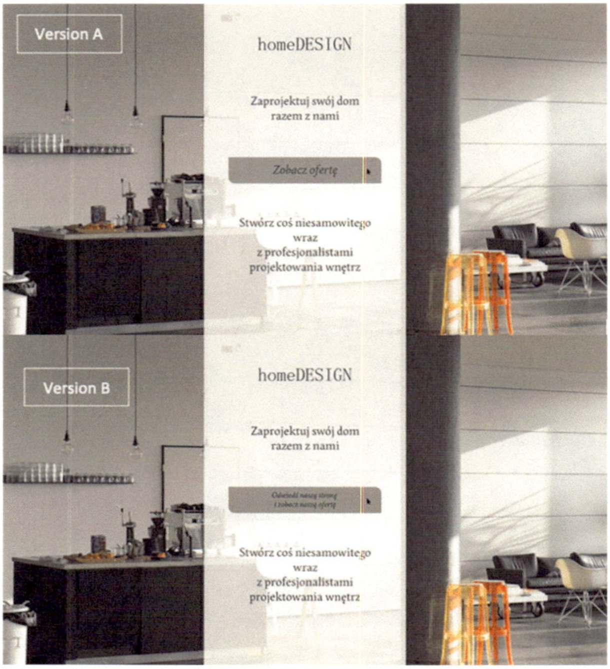

Figure 4.
Third pair of prototypes.

Figure 5.
Fourth Third pair of prototypes.

On the other hand, Version A is a more conservative version, probably appealing to a larger audience in general. Version B is the version for younger users who may have been exposed to the trend of neomorphism in many applications - it is nothing new or revelatory for them. It is more natural. It is worth noting that in the pairs of prototypes produced, it is impossible to determine which version is prettier clearly - this is a very subjective evaluation of each user. However, one can be guided by current design trends and user experience principles in such a way that one can determine which version is better and more functional. Also, notably, it included no dark pattern in the manufactured prototypes. Research on the manufactured prototypes is presented in the following subsection of the paper.

4. A/B testing analysis of the created landing page prototypes and surveys

Performed A/B testing of the created prototypes and surveys for testing. The purpose of A/B testing was to test the knowledge of the basic principles of website creation websites - in this case, landing pages - of users of different age groups and their personal preferences. The survey involved 451 users, including both men and women.

4.1 A/B tests

The user was allowed to make a single choice in the choice tests between two versions of the prototypes - versions A and B (**Figure 6**).

Figure 6.
Query in the test.

The command "Choose the version of the site that you think is better" has been specially constructed - so that the user does not suggest only one factor but the whole and complete site. Not necessarily just the appearance but also the functionality or a more modern approach to design. It assigned the command to each of the five pairs of prototypes.

4.2 Survey construction

The survey for A/B testing consisted of seven questions. Each question in the survey was mandatory and had clear answer guidelines - only one answer was always possible. The survey did not contain open-ended questions. It avoided answers that were not detailed enough or answers that were not relevant to the topic of the work.

The first question was a gender question, in which one could choose the "Female" and "Male" answers.

In addition, users were divided into four age groups:

- 10-22 years old - users who have been in contact with the Internet and computers since they were young and are mainly only familiar with the latest web design trends;
- 23-30 years old - users whose contact with the Internet and computer most likely began in their teenage years, having an idea of existing design trends in the early 21st century;
- 31-45 years old - users whose contact with the Internet and computer probably began in adulthood during their teenage years, who are definitively familiar with the design of Internet and computer content and trends of the early 21st century;
- 46+ years - users whose contact with the Internet began in adulthood are less likely to browse the web and are unfamiliar with today's trends and web design standards.

The next question asked about the frequency of Internet use. The question was asked in the form of a linear scale, from 1 to 5, where 1 - very rarely and 5 - very often. The amount of time spent, such as the answer "5 hours a day," was unnecessary in this question. What mattered was the user's subjective assessment, which made it clear whether they had daily contact with websites.

The next question was, "Do you often pay attention to the appearance of websites?" The answers were:

- "Yes, I pay attention to the appearance of websites; it is the most important."

- "I pay attention to the website's appearance, however, more to its functionality."
- "I pay attention to the appearance of the website to a moderate degree."
- "No, I don't pay complete attention to it."

Responses to this question in a later survey made it possible to divide users into those who pay more attention to the details of the sites, the esthetics, and those who are not influenced by the site's appearance—also tested familiarity with the concept of

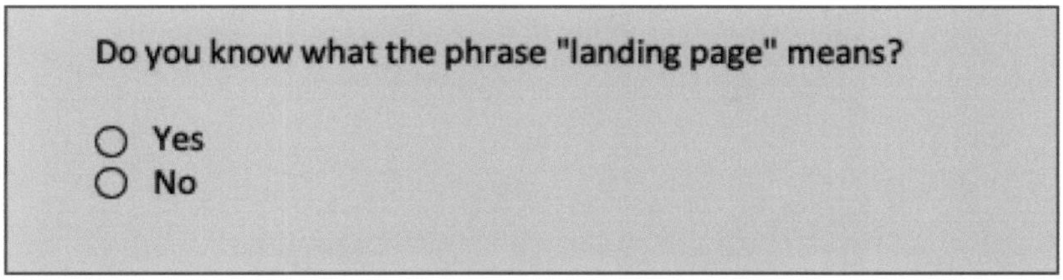

Figure 7.
Survey query for A/B testing.

a "landing page" during the survey execution. The next question was about this term - not everyone may have been familiar with it (**Figure 7**).

The next question in the survey was, "When performing A/B tests, did you pay attention to page details?" Possible answers to mark were:

- "I looked carefully before choosing an A or B version, e.g., font size and type, color scheme, etc."
- "I looked at the pages more generally, holistically, seeing some differences on them."
- "I didn't pay particular attention to the differences between versions A and B."

Since users can be divided here into visual and more interested, this is a fundamental question for the survey. This is because some users may not have noticed any differences between the A and B versions despite the specially selected order of prototypes in the A/B tests. Others, on the other hand, may have looked all too closely for some hidden content on the site after the first pair of prototypes without focusing on the site.

The last question was about performing A/B tests in the past. This question was strictly informational and did not change the subjective feelings about a particular pair of user prototypes. One can only assume that a user who had once performed such tests would approach the task more generally because he knew what to expect when performing the test.

5. Analysis and interpretation of the results of A/B tests of surveys

Simplified in work where the analysis and interpretation of data, A/B testing, and a survey through a single form via Google. This allowed us to see correlations between users' choices regarding their age, gender, or frequency of Internet use. The form was divided into the A/B tests and the survey. Completed the form by 451 people, including 180 men (39.9%) and 271 women (60,1%). 85 participants (18.8%) were aged 10–22, 148 participants (32.8%) were aged 23–30, 111 (24.6%) were aged 31–45, and 107 participants (23.7%) were over 46 years old. For the question "Do you often use the Internet?", where 1 is very rarely and 5 is very often, the number of respondents was as follows: 1–3 respondents (0.7%), 2–7 respondents (1.6%), 3–29 respondents (6.4%), 4–61 respondents (13.5%), 5–351 respondents (77.8%) (**Figure 8**).

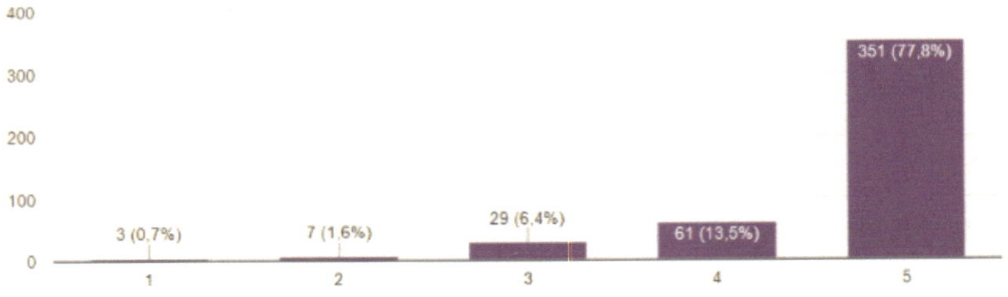

Figure 8.
Survey results relative to the frequency of Internet use.

About 67.6%, or 305 of those filling out the form, pay attention to the functionality of the site, not the look of it. In contrast, as many as 17.7%, or 80 respondents, believe that the website's appearance is the most important thing. 11.3%, or 51 respondents, focus only partially on the website's appearance. The rest, or 15 people (3.3%), do not focus on web design (**Figure 9**).

Of all respondents, as many as 55.2%, which equals 249 recipients, knew what a landing page was. The rest, 44.8%, 202 recipients, did not know the term (**Figure 10**).

Before choosing version A or version B, A/B testing of landing page prototypes was looked at by 274 people. They paid attention, for example, to the size of the fonts, their type, and the color scheme of the prototypes. 37.9% of the respondents, or 171 people, looked at the prototypes more holistically. However, they noted differences between the A and B versions. Only six individuals (1.3%) did not pay particular attention to the differences between the A and B versions.

Of those surveyed, as many as 241 had already performed A/B tests in the past (53.4%). The remaining 210 (46.6%) performed such tests for the first time (**Figure 11**).

For each pair of prototypes, the results were as follows:

- "Veggie's" - A version 11.5% (52 respondents), B version 88.5% (399 respondents) (**Figure 12**)

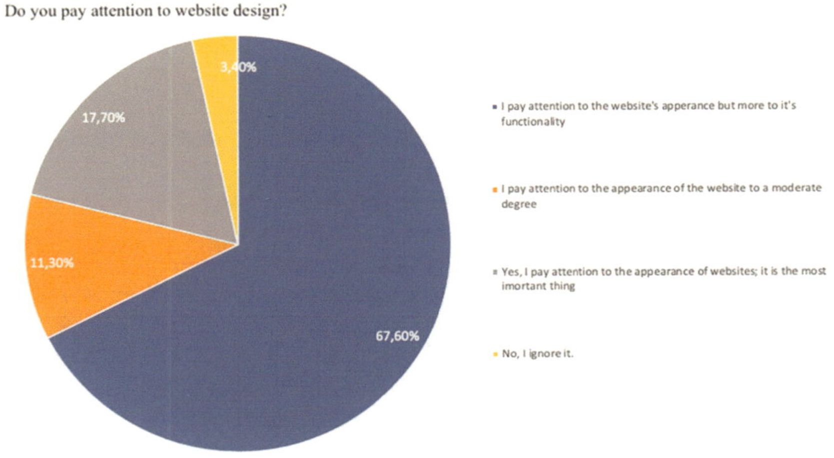

Figure 9.
Survey results relative to paying attention to website design.

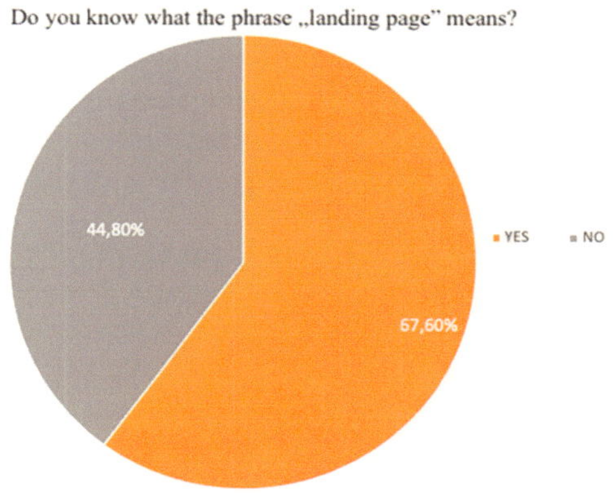

Figure 10.
Survey results on familiarity with the landing page concept.

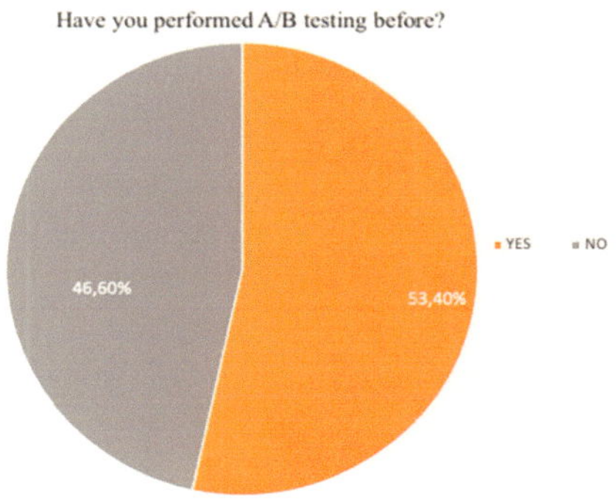

Figure 11.
Survey results on prior performance of A/B tests.

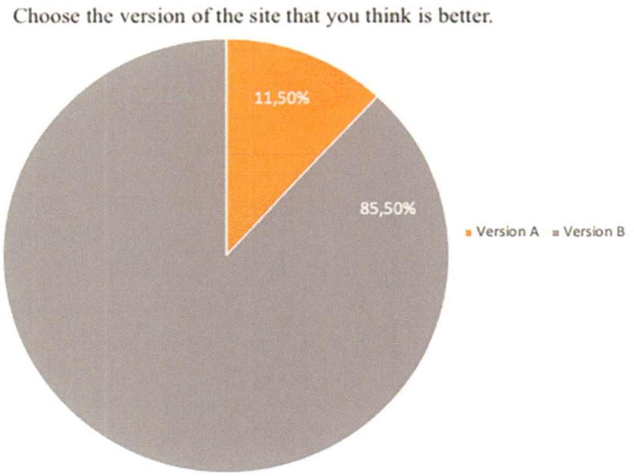

Figure 12.
A/B test results for a pair of prototypes "Veggie's".

The results by gender are as follows: For prototype one, 34 women chose version A (12.5% women), and as many as 237 women chose version B (87.5% women), whereas 18 men chose version A (10% men), while version B was chosen by 162 (90% men). This means that the results for the first pair of prototypes were very similar in percentage terms. There is no significant difference in gender with the first pair of prototypes.

- "hotelandresortspa.eu" - Version A 64.5% (291 respondents), version B 35.5% (160 respondents) (**Figure 13**)

In this pair of prototypes, as many as 168 women chose version A (62% women) and 103 version B (38% women). Men chose very similarly in percentage terms - 123 chose version A (68.3% of men) and 57 version B (31.7% of men).

- "homeDESIGN" - version A 86.5% (390 respondents), version B 13.5% (61 respondents) (**Figure 14**)

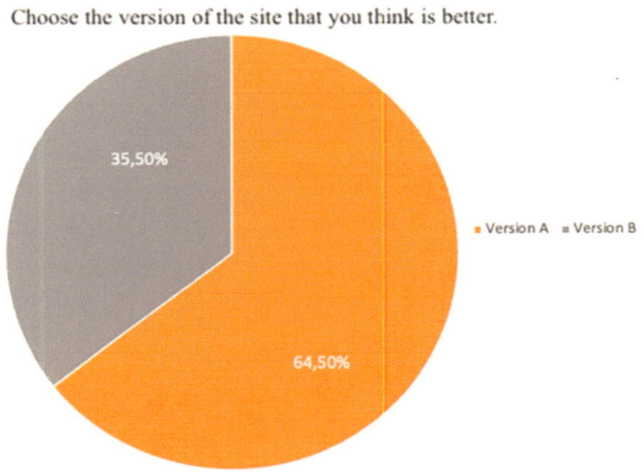

Figure 13.
A/B test results for a pair of prototypes "music.com".

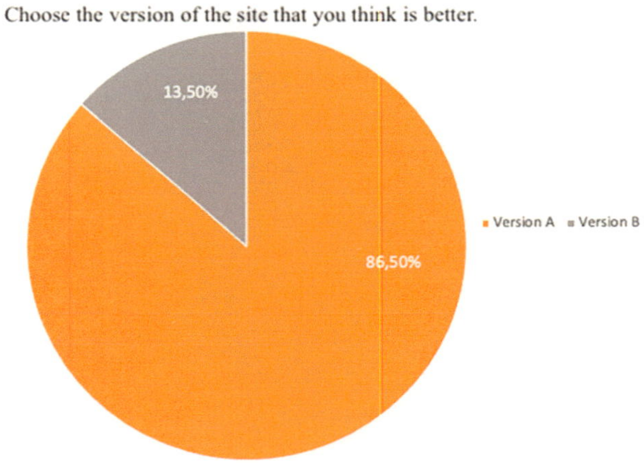

Figure 14.
A/B test results for a pair of prototypes "homeDESIGN".

In this pair of prototypes, there are slight differences in the choice between versions A and B regarding gender. As many as 227 women (83.8% women) chose version A, whereas 44 women (16.2% women) chose version B. 163 men (90.6% of men) chose version A, while the rest (9.4% of men) - 17 men - chose version B.

- "music.com"- A version 31% (140 respondents), B version 69% (311 respondents) (**Figure 15**)

In the last pair of prototypes, there were also no significant differences in the choice between the sexes. Women chose as follows: Version A by 83 women (30.6% of women), Version B by 188 women (69.4% of women). Among men, the results were as follows: 57 men chose version A (31.7% of men), while version B was chosen by 123 men (68.3% of men).

Because of the respondent's answers, the conclusion is that they prefer the appearance of prototypes that conform to generally accepted design principles 36 regardless of gender. The differences in the choices of the different versions were insignificant in the survey.

In the entire survey, a total of only 10 people very rarely or rarely (responses with values of 1 and 2) used the Internet. These included two men and eight women. All users, except for one woman in the 31–45 age category, were over 46 years old (**Figure 16**).

In **Figure 16**, we can see that three people chose "I pay moderate attention to the site's appearance," Four chose "I pay attention to the site's appearance, but more to its functionality," and the rest chose "No, I don't pay attention to it at all." In the first two pairs of prototypes by a majority (9 out of 10 votes), these people chose version B - the correct version in terms of user experience. In the third and fourth pairs of prototypes between versions A and B, the scores were 5 for both versions. In the fifth pair of prototypes, there were 4 A, and 6 B responses - the correct version here was B.

For the question "Did you pay attention to the details of the pages when doing A/B testing?" Six respondents did not pay particular attention to the differences in the prototypes. All of these people, except one in the 10–22 age group, were older than 46. Only three of them knew what a landing page was, including the person in the youngest age group.

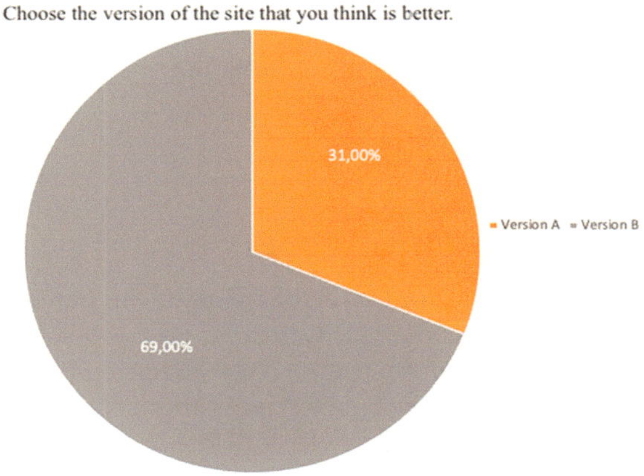

Figure 15.
A/B test results for a pair of prototypes.

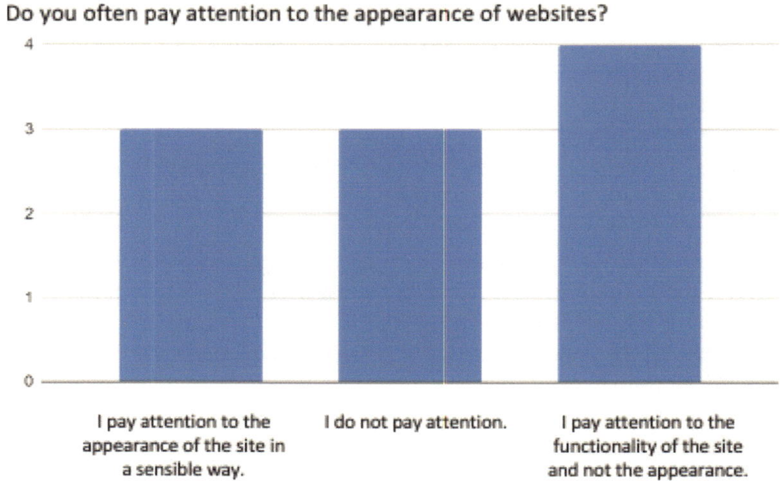

Figure 16.
Distribution of responses for very infrequent and infrequent use of the Internet in terms of paying attention to the appearance of websites.

In the question "Do you often pay attention to the appearance of websites?" many as 15 respondents do not pay attention. Only one of these people knew what a landing page was. These people also answered the frequency of Internet use - each gave a different answer from 1 to 5, in the same question, seven users. Interestingly - as many as 7 of these people answered, "I looked carefully before choosing the version they looked at before choosing version A or B, e.g., the size of the fonts and their type, color scheme, etc.". This indicates that they probably pay attention to the appearance of websites daily, however.

Additionally, in the question: Paying attention in the prototype to the details between versions A/B - 159 women (58.6% of all women) and 115 men (62.8% of all men) said they looked at the site closely before choosing the better version.

In contrast, in the general question: The appearance of websites - 49 women (18% of all women) and 31 men (17% of all men) believe that the look of a website is most important.

In addition, I calculated the mean and median for the Internet frequency rubric on a scale of 1 to 5. The mean was 4.66, while the median was 5. Thus, most users have constant contact with websites.

6. Conclusion

The paper presents an analysis and interpretation of the perception of website landing page prototypes and their templates created with Adobe software by users of different age groups based on user experience. The analysis presented shows that, depending on age, users have different preferences about the appearance of the websites in question. It is due to contact only with the latest design trends of younger people. Most likely, users have not all been exposed to other web design principles. From a young age, users are present with more **esthetically** pleasing websites. On the other hand, it's somewhat of a novelty for older users.

Due to the respondents' responses, the conclusion emerges that they mostly prefer the appearance of prototypes that conform to generally accepted design principles. The experiment shows that gender has little influence on this. It does, however, have the age and frequency of Internet use. Most users prefer when a site is **esthetically** pleasing but functional. Proved that in the age group over 46, the responses differed the most from generally accepted design principles relative to other age groups. The differences were up to 22%. Very often, in the 31–45 age group, the answers differed from those of the 10–22 and 23–30 age groups. These groups have been in contact with the Internet since childhood or teenage years. The differences here were also up to 20%. However, the responses of the 46+ age group differed the most on average in the five pairs of prototypes to other age groups.

The appearance of websites has changed dramatically over the years. Over time, sites have evolved both functionally and **esthetically**. Their main idea and concept have changed. Nowadays, content should no longer only be understandable to the user but also compressed to a minimum. They aim to convey the most relevant information with as little text as possible. This analysis can also help create and design landing pages to avoid bad practices while using good ones. Creating a correct landing page for any user, regardless of age, is difficult. Therefore, this work can serve as an educational resource for those beginning to design UX-compliant websites.

Author details

Luiza Fabisiak* and Barbara Jagielska
West Pomeranian University of Technology in Szczecin, Szczecin, Poland

*Address all correspondence to: lfabisiak@zut.edu.pl

References

[1] Ash T, Page R, Ginty M. Landing Page Optimization. Indianapolis: John Wiley & Sons; 2012. p. s.4

[2] Detante. 2022. [Internet] Available from: https://delante.pl/definicje/landing-page/. [Accessed: 17-05-2022]

[3] Wix Blog. 2022. [Internet] Available from: https://pl.wix.com/blog/artykul/tworzenie-landing-pages?utm_source=google&utm_medium=cpc&utm_campaign= 14050035777^133862885908&experiment_id=^^536052956531^^_DSA&gclid=CjwKCAjwj42UBhAAEiwACIhADgEjBrBsVbIdEvomxjvN_UNcGdHA3gnsgTaAkcsVIIobTPZ0PKcUhoCBOsQAvD_BwE#viewer-9blrs. [Accessed: 12.01.2022]

[4] Prodesigner. 2022. [Internet]. Available from: https://prodesigner.pl/co-to-jest-landing-page/. [Accessed: 17-12-2021]

[5] Marczak. 2022. [Internet]. Available from: https://marczak.me/efektywny-landing-page/#mcetoc_1d5c0ebdr3. [Accessed: 08-06-2022]

[6] Landingi. 2018. [Internet] Available from: https://landingi.com/pl/blog/4-techniki-optymalizacji-landing-page-potencjalnie-szkodzace-konwersji/. [Accessed: 17-05-2022]

[7] Raidboxes. 2019. [Internet] Available from: https://raidboxes.io/pl/blog/webdesign-development/typographie-grundlagen-webfonts-tipps/. [Accessed: 24-04-2019]

[8] Damianrams. 2019. [Internet]. Available from: https://www.damianrams.pl/landing-page/#8_dobrych_praktyk_w_tworzeniu_landing_page. [Accessed: 12-02-2019]

[9] Koduje. 2022. [Internet] Available from: https://www.koduje.pl/dostepne-materialy/dark-patterny-na-kodu-je. [Accessed: 23-05-2022]

[10] RekinySukcesu. 2022. [Internet] Available from: https://www.rekinysukcesu.pl/blog/internet/dark-patterns-czyli-ryzykowna-praktyka-ux. [Accessed: 20-07-2022]

[11] Netsolution. 2021. [Internet] Available from: https://www.netsolutions.com/insights/dark-patterns-in-ux-disadvantages/. [Accessed: 09-07-2021]

[12] Gray CM, Kou Y, Battles B, Hoggatt J, Toombs AL. The dark (patterns) side of UX design. In CHI 2018 - Extended Abstracts of the 2018 CHI Conference on Human factors in Computing Systems: Engage with CII (Conference on Human Factors in Computing Systems - Proceedings; Vol. 2018 - April). Association for Computing Machinery. DOI: 10.1145/3173574.3174108

[13] Gupta S, Kumaraguru P. Emerging Phishing Trends and Effectiveness of the Anti-Phishing Landing Page. Birmingham, IEEE; 2014. p. s. 39

[14] Marczak. 2021. [Internet] Available from: https://marczak.me/efektywny-landing-page/#mcetoc_1d5c0rjic7. [Accessed: 08-06-2021]

[15] Gofman A. Consumer driven multivariate landing page optimization: Overview, issues, and outlook. Transactions on Internet Research. 2007. p. 2. Available from: http://tir.ipsitransactions.org/2007/July/Paper%2003.pdf. [Accessed: 15-12-2022]

[16] Unbounce. 2021 [Internet] Available from: https://unbounce.com/page-speed-report/. [Accessed: 17-05-2022]

[17] Ash T, Page R, Ginty M. Landing Page Optimization. Indianapolis: John Wiley & Sons; 2012. p. s.31

[18] Landingi. 2022. [Internet] Available from: https://landingi.com/pl/tworzenie/landing-page/. [Accessed: 17-05-2022]

Chapter 3

Managing Quantities and Units of Measurement in Code Bases

Steve McKeever

Abstract

Quantities in engineering and the physical sciences are expressed as units of measurement (UoM). If a software system fails to maintain the algebraic attributes of a system's UoM information correctly when evaluating expressions then disastrous problems can arise. However, it is perhaps the more mundane unit mismatches and lack of interoperability that over time incurs a greater cost. Global and existential challenges, from infectious diseases to environmental breakdown, require high-quality data. Ensuring software systems support quantities explicitly is becoming less of a luxury and more of a necessity. While there are technical solutions that allow units of measurement to be specified at both the model and code level, a detailed assessment of their strengths and weaknesses has only recently been undertaken. This chapter provides both a formal introduction to managing quantities and a practical comparison of existing techniques so that software users can judge the robustness of their systems with regards to units of measurement.

Keywords: units of measurement, quantities, dimension checking, unit conversion, libraries, component based checking

1. Introduction

With ubiquitous digitalisation, and removal of humans in the loop, the need to faithfully represent and manipulate quantities in physical systems is ever increasing [1]. Popular programming languages allow developers to describe how to evaluate numeric expressions but not how to detect inappropriate actions on quantities. Consequently there have been infamous examples, such as the Mars Climate Orbiter [2], where units of measurement (UoM) conversion omissions led to catastrophic outcomes.

Humans have used local units of measurement since the days of early trade, enhanced over time to fulfil the accuracy and interoperable needs of science and technology. In the 19th century, James Clerk Maxwell [3] introduced the concept of a system of quantities with a corresponding system of units. This generalisation allowed scientists working with different measurement systems to communicate more easily, as unit names (such as inch or metre) are treated as numeric variables and can be interchanged through multiplication.

There are many ways in which manipulating physical quantities in a digital system can be made more robust. Thereby enabling the developer to depend on an automated validator, rather than trust, to ensure UoM are handled correctly. The software engineering benefits of embracing quantity checking and automatic conversion support is beyond dispute. It is clear from the various known UoM failures that one size does not fit all. However, a general lack of awareness has ensured that developers often reinvent the wheel or forego any kind of checking. From a correctness perspective, the optimal solution would be to natively support quantities as this allows for efficient unit conversion and static checking. However none of the mainstream languages provide such support, nor is that level of rigour always required. A software library might seem to confer the desired functionality of adding a unit type to one's preferred language but they are inconvenient in practice, adding an extra layer to one's code base, and incur a performance cost. All popular programming languages have a multitude of freely available quantity libraries but we argue that these are best suited to applications in which UoM checking is required at run-time. Component based checking and black-box testing are two lightweight methods of providing a degree of robustness while sacrificing completeness. Component checking will only validate the interfaces between components, while testing will ensure known examples of methods dealing with quantities perform correctly. Neither are comprehensive.

Implicit in our presentation is that the various approaches have compromises. For users who need a degree of robustness when using quantities in their code bases, this discussion is very important. An approach that initially might seem suitable for a given project, could be too costly in terms of speed, too cumbersome in terms of use or too risky by creating an unnecessary dependency on some library. In Section 2 we discuss early attempts to incorporate UoM checking into programming languages, and recent attempts to incorporate quantities into modelling languages. In Section 3 we introduce a very simple assignment language to show how the various aspects of quantities are defined and validated. In Section 4 we discuss the various approaches to providing quantity support in programming environments, highlighting their strengths and weaknesses. We summarise the results of our comparative study in Section 5, providing suggestions for developers as to which method to choose depending on their requirements, along with enabling software users to access pertinent aspects of an implementation that claims UoM support.

2. Background

Dimensions are physical quantities that can be measured, while units are arbitrary labels that correspond to a given dimension to make it relative. For example a dimension is length, whereas a `metre` is a relative unit that describes length. Units of measure can be defined in the most generic form as either *base quantities* or *derived quantities*. The base quantities are the basic building blocks, and the derived quantities are built from these. For instance, the base quantity for time is `second` and that for length is `metre` in the International System of Units (SI), also known as the metric system. The SI system of measurement is based on seven base quantities for length, mass, time, electric current, temperature, quantity, and brightness [4]. Velocity, ($\mathsf{metre/second}$ or $\mathsf{metre} \times \mathsf{second}^{-1}$), is a derived quantity made from the two base quantities. Rather than representing UoM as a tree structure, a normal form exists which makes storage and comparison a lot easier. Any system of units can be derived from the base units as a product of powers of those base units: $\mathsf{base}^{e_1} \times \mathsf{base}^{e_2} \times \ldots \mathsf{base}^{e_n}$, where the exponents

$e_1,...,e_n$ are rational numbers. Thus an SI unit can be represented as a 7-tuple $(e_1, ..., e_7)$ where e_i denotes the i-th base unit; or in our case e_1 denotes length, e_2 mass, e_3 time and so on.

Adding units to conventional programming languages originates in the 1970s [5] and early 80s with proposals to extend Fortran [6] and then Pascal [7]. However these efforts were heavily syntax based and required modifications to the underlying languages, reducing backwards compatibility and thus uptake. Ada's abstraction facilities, namely operator overloading and type parameterisation, allowed for a more versatile approach [8] to labelling variables with UoM features. With the appearance of practical object oriented programming languages, such as C++ and Java, developers began to implement UoM either by means of a class hierarchy of units and their derived forms, or via the Quantity pattern [9]. This has led to a veritable explosion in the number of UoM libraries available for all popular programming languages based on this pattern [10].

Software development typically begins at a more abstract level through diagrams and rules that focus on the conceptual model that is to be implemented. Extensions to the Unified Modelling Language (UML) have been proposed to support quantities. SysML, for instance, is defined as an extension of a subset of UML to support systems engineering activities and has extensive support for quantities[1]. Unit checking and conversion can be undertaken before code is generated, either through a compilation workflow that leverages Object Constraint Language (OCL) expressions [11] or staged computation [12]. Unless the workflow has been created specifically, declaring quantities in a system specification language offers no guarantee that the UoM information is supported in the eventual implementation. The aim of this chapter is to discuss the various ways in which quantity information can be transferred into software and errors detected either at compile-time or run-time. Motivated by a prior critique of UoM libraries and a survey of scientific coders [13], we assess various approaches based on their ease of use, execution speed, numeric accuracy, ease of integration and coverage of unit error detection capabilities.

We lack a definitive understanding of how frequently quantity errors occur in practice. Anecdotally we can infer that it is not negligible from experiments described in the literature. When applied to a repository of CellML models, a validation tool [14] found that 60% of the descriptions that were invalid had dimensionally inconsistent units. A spreadsheet checker [15] was applied to 22 published scientific spreadsheets and detected 3, nearly 14%, with errors. Ore [16] applied his lightweight C++ unit inconsistency tool to 213 open-source systems, finding inconsistencies in 11% of them. It must be noted that these figures are gleaned from post development studies and are not representative of a quantity adhering software discipline. Thus, it seems important to ensure UoM information existing in software models is supported in derived implementations.

3. Validating quantities

Performing calculations in relation to quantities, dimensions and units is subtle and can easily lead to mistakes. We shall begin by looking at a very simple language of declarations and assignments so that we can untangle the various aspects involved in

[1] https://sysml.org

$$
\begin{array}{lcl}
\mathcal{E} : uexp \rightarrow (uv \rightarrow value) \rightarrow value & & \\
\mathcal{E}[\![uv]\!]_\rho & = & \rho\ uv \\
\mathcal{E}[\![uexp_1 + uexp_2]\!]_\rho & = & \mathcal{E}[\![uexp_1]\!]_\rho + \mathcal{E}[\![uexp_2]\!]_\rho \\
\mathcal{E}[\![r * uexp]\!]_\rho & = & r \times \mathcal{E}[\![uexp]\!]_\rho \\
\mathcal{E}[\![uexp_1 * uexp_2]\!]_\rho & = & \mathcal{E}[\![uexp_1]\!]_\rho \times \mathcal{E}[\![uexp_2]\!]_\rho
\end{array}
$$

Figure 1.
Rules for evaluating expressions.

managing quantities correctly. A program will consist of a sequence of UoM variable declarations, *uv*, followed by a sequence of assignment statements, *ustmt*. Unit arithmetic expressions, *uexp*, impose syntactic restrictions so that their soundness can be inferred using the algebra of quantities.

$$
\begin{array}{lcl}
ustmt & := & uv := uexp \\
uexp & := & uv \mid uexp_1 + uexp_2 \mid r * uexp \mid uexp_1 * uexp_2
\end{array}
$$

By creating a separate syntax for unit expressions we can distinguish between scalar values, such as *r*, and *unitless quantities* in which all the dimensions are zero, such as moisture content. Consider a simple program to calculate Newton's second law of motion:

```
begin
  f : float;
  m : float of 5.7;
  a : float of 3.2;
  ...
  f : = m * a
end
```

We can use the evaluate function, $\mathcal{E}$ of **Figure 1**, with an environment consisting of values for m and a to calculate f:

$$
\begin{array}{lcl}
\mathcal{E}[[\mathrm{m} * \mathrm{a}]]_{\{\mathrm{m}\mapsto 5.7,\ \mathrm{a}\mapsto 3.2\}} & = & \mathcal{E}[[\mathrm{m}]]_{\{\mathrm{m}\mapsto 5.7,\ \mathrm{a}\mapsto 3.2\}} \times \mathcal{E}[[\mathrm{a}]]_{\{\mathrm{m}\mapsto 5.7,\ \mathrm{a}\mapsto 3.2\}} \\
& = & (\{\mathrm{m}\mapsto 5.7,\ \mathrm{a}\mapsto 3.2\}\ \mathrm{m}) \times (\{\mathrm{m}\mapsto 5.7,\ \mathrm{a}\mapsto 3.2\}\ \mathrm{a}) \\
& = & 5.7 \times 3.2
\end{array}
$$

As is the case in nearly all programming languages, users have to assume that the mass (m) is given in kilograms, and the acceleration (a) is given in metres per second per second for the assignment to be correct. The reminder of this section explores the various aspects involved in handling quantities correctly, and how these aspects can be automated.

3.1 Dimensions

A dimensional analysis needs to ensure that (1) two physical quantities can only be equated if they have the same dimensions; (2) two physical quantities can only be added if they have the same dimensions (known as the *Principle of Dimensional Homogeneity*); (3) the dimensions of the multiplication of two quantities is given by the addition of the dimensions of the two quantities. If we only consider the three

$$
\begin{array}{lcl}
\mathcal{DE} : uexp \rightarrow (uv \rightarrow dims) \rightarrow dims & & \\
\mathcal{DE}[\![uv]\!]_\varrho & = & \varrho\, uv \\
\mathcal{DE}[\![uexp_1 + uexp_2]\!]_\varrho & = & \mathcal{DE}[\![uexp_1]\!]_\varrho \mathbin{\hat{+}} \mathcal{DE}[\![uexp_2]\!]_\varrho \\
\mathcal{DE}[\![r * uexp]\!]_\varrho & = & \mathcal{DE}[\![uexp]\!]_\varrho \\
\mathcal{DE}[\![uexp_1 * uexp_2]\!]_\varrho & = & \mathcal{DE}[\![uexp_1]\!]_\varrho \mathbin{\hat{\times}} \mathcal{DE}[\![uexp_2]\!]_\varrho
\end{array}
$$

Figure 2.
Dimensional analysis rules for expressions.

common dimensions of length, mass and time then we can capture the rules for addition and multiplication.

$$
\begin{array}{lcl}
(l_1, m_1, t_1) \mathbin{\hat{+}} (l_2, m_2, t_2) & = & (l_1, m_1, t_1), \text{ if } l_1 = l_2 \wedge m_1 = m_2 \wedge t_1 = t_2 \\
(l_1, m_1, t_1) \mathbin{\hat{\times}} (l_2, m_2, t_2) & = & (l_1 + l_2, m_1 + m_2, t_1 + t_2)
\end{array}
$$

This allows us to rewrite the rules of **Figure 1** by replacing the addition and multiplication operators to create a dimensional checker, shown in **Figure 2**. Scalar multiplication does not affect the dimensions of a quantity. The dimension of mass, `m`, is described as (0,1,0), while acceleration is `length` × `time`$^{-2}$, or (1,0,-2) as a tuple. Our dimensional checker will compute with dimensions and attempt to ensure all assignments are correct. Consider our example program:

```
begin
  f : float of (1,1,-2);
  m : float of (0,1,0);
  a : float of (1,0,-2);
  ...
  f : = m * a
end
```

Checking would proceed as follows:

$$
\begin{array}{l}
\mathcal{DE}[[\mathrm{m} * \mathrm{a}]]_{\{\mathrm{m}\mapsto(0,1,0),\ \mathrm{a}\mapsto(1,0,-2)\}} \\
\quad = \mathcal{DE}[[\mathrm{m}]]_{\{\mathrm{m}\mapsto(0,1,0),\ \mathrm{a}\mapsto(1,0,-2)\}} \mathbin{\hat{\times}} \mathcal{DE}[[\mathrm{a}]]_{\{\mathrm{m}\mapsto(0,1,0),\ \mathrm{a}\mapsto(1,0,-2)\}} \\
\quad = (\{\mathrm{m}\mapsto(0,1,0),\ \mathrm{a}\mapsto(1,0,-2)\}\ \mathrm{m}) \mathbin{\hat{\times}} (\{\mathrm{m}\mapsto(0,1,0),\ \mathrm{a}\mapsto(1,0,-2)\}\ \mathrm{a}) \\
\quad = (0,1,0) \mathbin{\hat{\times}} (1,0,-2) \\
\quad = (1,1,-2)
\end{array}
$$

and as this dimension matches `f` we know that the assignment is correct. Most UoM checkers adopt this approach, extending the checking into the statements and function calls of typical programming language constructs. For instance, all branches of conditionals and case statements must have the same dimensions, while comparison operators can only operate on quantities of the same dimension. If the dimensions of all variables are known at compile-time then this process can be undertaken before the program runs.

3.2 Kinds of quantities

Two values that share the same UoM might not represent the same *kinds of quantities* (KOQ) [17]. For example, torque is a rotational force which causes an object to rotate about an axis while work is the result of a force acting over some distance. Surface tension can be described as newtons per meter or kilogram per second squared, and even though they equate, they represent different quantities.

We have recently developed a simple set of rules for arithmetic and function calls that allow quantities to be named and handled *safely* [18]. This is not as straightforward as preserving the names of quantities throughout the program text. Multiplication will generate a new quantity so it is very likely that information is lost in intermediate stages of a calculation. Moreover, not all quantity variables in a program will have a name such as Torque or Work. Some might denote an entity such as length that could be in metres or yards, while another might be a variable used to store some temporary value. Neither of these need to be named. Using an algebraic data type, we define named quantities as:

$$\texttt{type quantname} = \texttt{Named of string} \mid \texttt{No name}$$

We can now define the rules for adding and multiplying named quantities. In both cases we assume that the unit expression is dimensionally correct, our concern is to define how named quantities conduct themselves. The operator $\diamond$ takes two named quantities and states the conditions under which they can be summed: *two named quantities can be added together only if they represent the same entity*, if one quantity is named but the other is not then it is necessary for the result to be named, and if both are unnamed then the result will be too:

$$\begin{array}{lcl} \texttt{Named}\ n_1 \diamond \texttt{Named}\ n_2 & = & \texttt{Named}\ n_1, \quad \text{if } n_1 = n_2 \\ \texttt{Named}\ n \diamond \texttt{Noname} & = & \texttt{Named}\ n \\ \texttt{Noname} \diamond \texttt{Named}\ n & = & \texttt{Named}\ n \\ \texttt{Noname} \diamond \texttt{Noname} & = & \texttt{Noname} \end{array}$$

Our comparison rules cast upwards from Noname to Named, so as to assume a named quantity whenever possible. This is required to ensure named quantities behave correctly. For multiplication the rules are simpler. The operator Δ takes in two named quantities and defines how they behave over the multiplication operator. As *multiplication sums the dimensions of the two operands, the value will be different to either and so the result will always be* $\_\Delta\_$ = Noname. The rules for named quantity analysis of expressions are given in **Figure 3**.

Multiplication will generate a new quantity so it is very likely that information is lost in intermediate stages of a calculation. We propose that functions, whose return KOQ are known, are used to regain information when calculations use multiplication.

$$\begin{array}{lcl} \multicolumn{3}{l}{\mathcal{NE} : uexp \to (uv \to \texttt{quantname}) \to \texttt{quantname}} \\ \mathcal{NE}[\![uv]\!]_\tau & = & \tau\ uv \\ \mathcal{NE}[\![uexp_1 + uexp_2]\!]_\tau & = & \mathcal{NE}[\![uexp_1]\!]_\tau \diamond \mathcal{NE}[\![uexp_2]\!]_\tau \\ \mathcal{NE}[\![r * uexp]\!]_\tau & = & \mathcal{NE}[\![uexp]\!]_\tau \\ \mathcal{NE}[\![uexp_1 * uexp_2]\!]_\tau & = & \mathcal{NE}[\![uexp_1]\!]_\tau \vartriangle \mathcal{NE}[\![uexp_2]\!]_\tau \end{array}$$

Figure 3.
Named quantity rules for unit expression.

In this manner a discipline of programming with quantities is suggested Nonetheless, we can exemplify how our approach behaves on a simple incorrect assignment where we try to add a value of torque to one of work:

```
begin
   sumt : float of Named Torque;
   t : float of Named Torque;
   w : float of Named of Work;
   ...
   sumt : = t + w
end
```

Checking would start as follows:

$$\begin{aligned} &\mathcal{NE}[[\mathtt{t}+\mathtt{w}]]_{\{\mathrm{t}\mapsto \mathrm{Named\ \ Torque,\ w}\mapsto \mathrm{Named\ \ Work}\}} \\ &= \mathcal{NE}[[\mathrm{t}]]_{\{\mathrm{t}\mapsto \mathrm{Named\ \ Torque,\ w}\mapsto \mathrm{Named\ \ Work}\}} \diamond \mathcal{NE}[[w]]_{\{\mathrm{t}\mapsto \mathrm{Named\ \ Torque,\ w}\mapsto \mathrm{Named\ \ Work}\}} \\ &= (\{\mathrm{t}\mapsto \mathrm{Named\ \ Torque,\ \ w}\mapsto \mathrm{Named\ \ Work})\}\ \mathrm{t}) \\ &\diamond\ (\{\mathrm{t}\mapsto \mathrm{Named\ \ Torque,\ \ w}\mapsto \mathrm{Named\ \ Work}\}\ \mathrm{w}) \\ &= \mathrm{NamedTorque}\ \diamond\ \mathrm{NamedWork} \end{aligned}$$

and as we cannot proceed, we deduce that the assignment is unsafe. None of the current methodologies for managing quantities perform this kind of quantity checking.

3.3 Systems of Units

Dimension analysis would be sufficient if only one unit system, such as the SI system, was required. In such cases the base units of metre, gram and second could be implicit in implementations. There are, however, two further complications. A system of units provides a set of base units but they can be extended with prefixes. For instance, the SI system allows lengths to be described in terms of the base unit metre and prefixes, such as kilo- and centi-. While the Imperial system has the base unit feet on which an inch and a yard are constructed. Consequently we need to consider normalising values within a system of units and allow dimensionally faithful expressions to evaluate correctly with different units of measurement, as shown in **Figure 4**.

3.3.1 Normalising within a system of units

We can extend our tuple for dimensions to include prefixes. They are used to avoid very large or very small numeric values. Speed is typically shown in kilometres per hour, which we could represent in our 3-tuple as `((kilometre,1),(gram,0),(hour,-1))`. This approach simplifies normalisation. A kilometre can be converted into metres by multiplying the value by a 1000, and an hour is 3600 seconds. Consider the dimensionally correct assignment below where the mass, m, is given in grams:

```
begin
   f : float of ((metre,1),(kilogram,1),(second,-2));
   m : float of ((metre,0),(gram,1),(second,0));
   a : float of ((metre,1),(gram,0),(second,-2));
   ...
   f : = m * a
end
```

A UoM analysis would reveal that force, f, is expected in Newtons so the value for m needs to be divided by 1000, f:= (m/1000)*a. It is straightforward to normalise within a given system of units by aligning the prefixes. However, we also need to take the exponent into account. For example, the density of iron is 7.86 g/cm^3, and can be converted into kg/m^3 as follows:

$$\begin{aligned}&7.86 \times (\mathcal{C}\ \ (\text{gram},\ \ \text{kilogram})) \times (\mathcal{C}\ \ (\text{centimetre},\ \ \text{metre}))^{-3}\\&= 7.86 \times 0.001 \times 0.01^{-3}\\&= 7860\ \ kg/m^3\end{aligned}$$

where we assume the existence of a function $\mathcal{C}$ that takes in two prefixes and returns the conversion factor.

3.3.2 Converting between two Systems of Units

A second issue is that of converting in-between two systems of units. This can be achieved by extending the function $\mathcal{C}$ to convert between known systems, such as from yards to metres and visa-versa. Consider a similar example to the Mars climate orbiter error, here we want to calculate momentum, where p is mass times velocity, in Newton seconds, or $m{\cdot}Kg{\cdot}s^{-1}$. However our mass is in pounds:

```
begin
  p : float of ((metre,1),(kilogram,1),(second,-1));
  m : float of ((metre,0),(pound,1),(second,0));
  v : float of ((metre,1),(gram,0),(second,-1));
  ...
  p : = m * v
end
```

The function conversion, $\mathcal{C}$ (pound, kilogram), yields 0.45 so we need to modify the assignment so that the result will be correct, namely p := 0.45*m*v.

A naive unit conversion algorithm will convert the right hand side's units to the left hand side's for each sub-expression when performing addition or multiplication, but this is rarely the most efficient. The algorithm described by Cooper [14] is applied at compile-time. It choose the least number of conversions by generating all possible valid UoM conversions from a given expression, and selecting the one with the fewest conversions. Finally, many non-SI units continue to be used in the scientific, technical, and commercial literature. Some units are deeply rooted in history and culture.

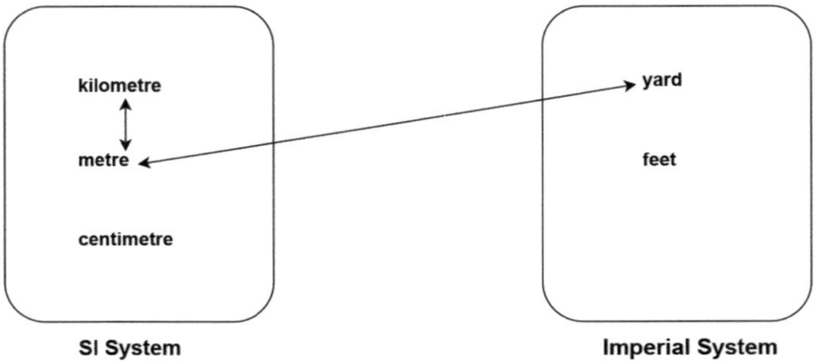

Figure 4.
Conversion within and in-between systems of units.

We use the term week rather than 168 hours. These also need to be supported through conversion functions.

3.4 Levels of measurement

A further aspect is that of the operations that might be applicable to a given quantity. To a physicist or applied mathematician, it is taken for granted that a quantity is used in the same manner as a unit-independent value, and that all arithmetic and comparative operators can be applied to it. However this is often not the case. For instance, what operations apply to a person's IQ? It does not makes sense to multiply scales of intelligence or personality traits.

Stevens [19] identified four categories of scale that places limits on the type of measurement that can be used to construct valid terms:

1. *Nominal Scales* represents the most unrestricted assignment of numerals. The only operations that applies to values in a nominal scale is that of *equality* and *inequality*, essentially numerals are only used as labels.

2. *Ordinal Scales* permits rank ordering. The classic example of an ordinal scale is the scale of hardness of minerals. Most of the scales used by psychologists are ordinal scales. Operations such as *greater-than* and *less-than* are also applicable to ordinal scales. In the strictest sense, statistical operations involving means and standard deviations should not to be used with these scales as they imply a knowledge of something more than the rank order of data. This is due to the successive intervals on the scale being unequal in size but the 'illegal' application of statistical functions is often very useful, such as the average IQ of a certain population.

3. *Interval Scales* are what we would consider quantitative and allow *addition* and *subtraction*, so all the usual statistical measures are applicable. The zero point on an interval scale is a matter of convention. Centigrade and Fahrenheit both represent volumes of expansion, with an arbitrary zero for each scale, such that a numerical value on one scale can be converted into a value on the other.

4. *Ratio Scales* are most commonly encountered in physics and include the previous three relations, along with *multiplication* and *division*. An absolute zero is always implied.

Currently no system employs levels of measurement checking, such that only meaningful operations are applied to certain quantities. We suspect that this is due to even less awareness of scale levels and an assumption that quantity checking is only necessary for ratio scales. Hall [20] has developed a UML class diagram that captures the inheritance relationship between the four levels, enabling operations to be restricted to the most general of a pair of operands. As discussed with the ordinal scale, there is a pragmatic context that needs to be considered when using levels of measurement.

3.5 Summary of quantity checking

Through the use of an illustrative expression language we have shown how to ensure programs correctly manipulate the dimensions, the named quantities and the

UoM of values. In doing so we have raised two important issues relating to the implementation of quantities: at what point checking and conversions can occur, and how extensive the coverage will be. If all UoM variables are annotated, or their annotations inferred, then both dimension checking and unit conversions can be undertaken by the compiler. This means that programs with UoM errors will be detected early, before the system is put in place, creating a strongly UoM typed language. Moreover, the code can be optimised so as to have the least number of conversions, reducing rounding errors, and increasing the accuracy of its calculations. The technique can be extended to include assertions on allowable unit conversions. If UoM are only known at run-time, or their design is embedded within the host language, then dimension checking and unit conversions will be undertaken at run-time. Programs will still manipulate UoM correctly but with a performance penalty and errors will only be detected once running. One must also consider the annotation burden, [21] found subjects choose a correct UoM annotation only 51% of the time and take an average of 136 seconds to make a single correct annotation.

4. Implementing quantities

Many constructs in Software Models can be directly translated into code. A UML class diagram can be used to build the class structure of an object oriented implementation. The situation for UoM annotations is more complex. UoM values are neither primitive nor reference types in modern object oriented terminology. As described in Section 3, they require an advanced checker to ensure variables and method calls are handled soundly by the compiler.

In this Section we shall look at the four practical methods that support unit checking of code basis. All implementation options are affected by the following three concerns [13]: *lack of awareness*, *cumbersome implementations* and *lack of support* from the given software eco-system. Software rarely lives in a vacuum so even if it has been designed and developed with one of these methods, associated components are unlikely to support UoM, such as legacy libraries, databases and spreadsheets. Nonetheless as sources of data are migrated to quantity aware formats, the software must be able to follow suit.

4.1 Native language support

Adding unit checking to conventional imperative, object-oriented and even functional languages using syntactic sugaring is beyond the algorithmic scope of their underlying type checkers. The pioneering foundational work of Wand and O'Keefe [22] demonstrated how the simply-typed lambda calculus could be extended with dimensions. Milner's polymorphic type inference algorithm [23] is symbolic, so in order to include UoM variable resolution one has to provide an equational solver based on the theory of Abelian groups [24]. A programming language with native support will include additional syntax for UoM and an enhanced static analyser that calculates or infers the validity of annotations. When UoM annotations are validated prior to compilation, errors can be detected early and generated arithmetic code can minimise the number of conversions, mitigating round-off errors.

The only language in the 20 most popular programming languages [25] that supports units of measurement is Apple's Swift language [26]. Microsoft's F# [27] is a general purpose functional language with a full implementation of UoM, including unit variables that the static checker will seek to determine at compile-time [24]. This property permits valid UoM programmes to be written in which not all the quantity variables are annotated, thereby reducing the annotation burden and allowing greater reusability. However, large software projects rarely use either Swift or F#.

4.1.1 C++ boost library

C++ is still very popular [25] and has a de facto UoM extension that exploits the template meta-programming feature[2]. Consequently BoostUnits is more than just a library as it supports a staged computation model, similar to MixGen [12], which has the benefit of providing a language extension while still supporting backwards compatibility. C++ is quite unique in terms of being a popular programming language that supports this adaptable compilation strategy. Dimensional analysis is treated as a generic compile-time meta-programming problem, and delivers features and performance comparable to native language support. As no run-time penalty is incurred, BoostUnits supports UoM checking in performance-critical code. However, the survey [28] found both usability and accuracy issues with the use of this library.

4.1.2 Unit of measurement validators

Creating a new compiler feature for an existing language is contentious, non-trivial and likely to become outmoded. An alternative static approach is to define UoM through comments or attributes and to build a tool that attempts to perform as much scrutiny as possible. Such a validator checks at compile-time for unit violations without adding a new syntax or changing the run-time behaviour of the code. **Figure 5** shows an example of the Unit of Measurement Validator for C# [29]. The Osprey [30]

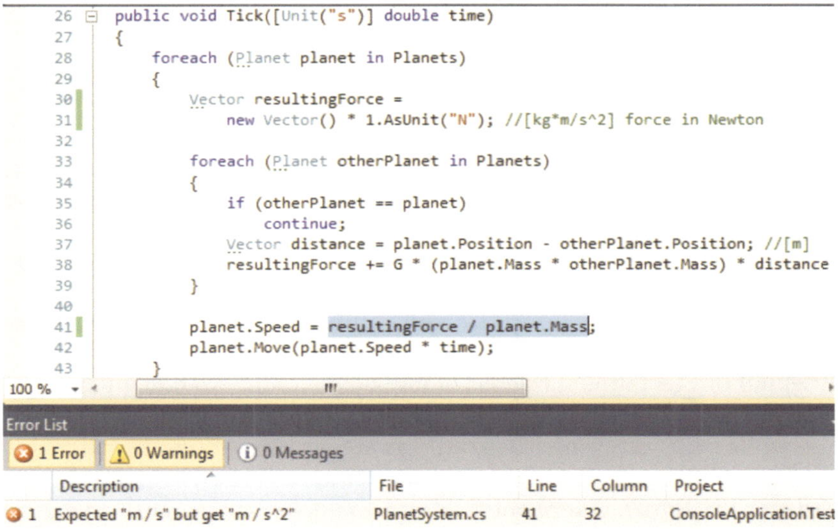

Figure 5.
Example of unit of measurement validator for C#.

[2] https://github.com/boostorg/units

system is a C front end that automatically checks for all potential quantity errors. UoM are annotated with a $ and are modelled as types, reducing dimensional analysis to type checking, with Gaussian elimination to resolve unspecified UoM variable exponents. Simiarly [31] allows one to express relationships between the units of function parameters and return values. Ensuring the validity of unit conversions can be specified. PUnits [32] is a Java front end, or pluggable type system, that has many additional features. It can be used in three modes: checking the correctness of a program, solving UoM type variables, and annotating a program with units. This last feature is the most novel and allows human inspection which is useful since having a valid typing does not guarantee that the inferred specification expresses design intent, and allows KOQs to be expressed. These approaches are lightweight and scalable but they need to be supported for users to feel that they are credible. Alas few of these tools have lifespans outside of their original research project.

4.1.3 Domain-specific languages (DSLs) with quantities

DSLs are languages specialised to a particular application domain. They are often written in a mark-up language such as XML or JSON which facilitates their use with general purpose languages as they can be easily parsed. They might have originally been designed for the purpose of curation, such as CellML and SMBL where the intention was to build biological repositories of computational models. A model will include the constants, variables and equations denoting a particular biological system. Thus, translating them into a programming language with the aid of a differential equation solver means that they can be readily simulated [33]. If the DSL contains UoM declarations then separately analysing source files can be undertaken before they are uploaded to a repository and translated into the run-time system [14]. Quantity checking coverage might be limited to the application domain but one can easily make the argument that this is where the vulnerabilities would lie.

4.2 Static or dynamic library support

Adding a feature to an existing programming language is usually undertaken by developing a library which implements the desired behaviour. It is written in terms of the language, using advanced abstraction methods such as classes and generics, and delivers a well-defined interface. There are many UoM libraries for all modern programming languages [34]. The basic idea behind dimensional analysis, as shown in Section 3.1, is relatively straightforward and familiar to scientific coders. However, *"making a physical quantity library is easy but making a good one is hard"* [35]. The reasons behind this lie in the subtleties of implementation: providing non-standard UoM, offering many new operators, supporting conversions, creating helpful error messages, while being efficient. These aspects are far harder to code and maintain than a faithful implementation of the Quantity pattern [9, 36].

Experience has shown that quantity libraries add an extra layer to an existing application through boilerplate code that is rarely idiomatic to the host language. The Quantity pattern ensures that values are hard-wired to have a single floating point representation, requiring further conversions to other internal formats and accuracy issues. Poor error messages are also a frequent complaint. Certain modern languages, such as Ruby, provide a special syntax for adding features to the language which exploit duck typing, enabling lightweight libraries to be built. The main conclusion is that for adoption to occur, UoM must be included in such a way that they are almost as easy to use as standard arithmetic types [13].

The standard technique for implementing the Quantity pattern is through exploiting overriding, making UoM checking a run-time activity. However UoM can be implemented through static overloading, or Java generic instantiations, ensuring compile-time checking. An example of both styles is shown in [13]. Merging the two techniques would double the amount of notation required and significantly add to the burden of adoption. Languages such as Python or Ruby are dynamically typed by definition, so quantity checking will occur at run-time regardless of how UoM are defined. Run-time support is a key reason why there are so many libraries for these two languages when typically one would assume quantities require high-performance executables. From a user survey of UoM libraries: *"In our product line, our users may very well have one file whose units are 'kg · m*^{3}*', another whose units are 'g_cc'and a third whose units are 'degrees Celsius'. We therefore need to be able to operate on units at run-time, not compile-time"* [28].

An additional limitation of libraries versus a native language or a pluggable type solution is that variables of a Quantity class can be reassigned at run-time. The 7-tuple that represents dimensions can be modified such that a kilometre could become a newton. Dimensional homogeneity and conversion errors can be caught by a library implementation but to avoid such programming style errors necessitates discipline. A dimensionally aware static checker ensures that all instances of a quantity declaration have the same dimensions. Errors caused by this violation were found to account for 75% of inconsistencies in the study of 5.9 M lines of code [37].

Implementing UoM through a data type or a class requires values to be boxed at run-time, incurring both speed and memory penalties. Native language solutions can perform the checking at compile-time so that generated executables contain no further UoM annotations and values are represented by primitive types. For scientific applications that perform many calculations, such as matrix multiplications, this unnecessary performance overhead is unacceptable. A UoM library might seem attractive and undemanding initially, but the subtle burden that they inflict will often increase the complexity of a project.

4.3 Component or Interface description support

Encapsulating implementation details, interfaces are a collection of the externally visible entities and function signatures of a component. They are used by the compiler to ensure access is handled correctly. Libraries, native language support and pluggable type systems usually require all quantity variable and function declarations to have UoM annotations, while component or interface based approaches only require certain functions to be annotated. This drastically reduces the annotation burden, supports legacy code but at the expense of robustness.

A component based approach seeks to add UoM information to the interface in order to enforce unit consistency when composing components and thereby reduce dimensional mismatch errors. There is some anecdotal evidence in the many quotes of [28] to support this approach. Damevski [38] hypothesises that UoM libraries are too restricting by requiring complete coverage, incurring an annotation or migration burden. His technique performs dimensional analysis on component interfaces at run-time, and if the calling parameters are compatible with the arguments dimensions then unit conversions occur. Consider the C++ class Earth [38]:

```
class Earth {.
    void setCircumference(in Metre circumference);
    Metre getCircumference();
}
```

It assigns and queries the earth's circumference using `Metre` internally but can be called with `Kilometre` and the return value bound to a variable of, say, type `Mile`. Unlike libraries, within the class `Earth` no further annotations are required, nor will internal declarations be checked. This is a dynamic component based approach, units are converted at run-time.

Another lightweight methodology was presented by Ore [16] which performs an initial pass to build a table mapping attributes in C++ shared libraries to UoM. The shared libraries have been specifically enhanced to include UoM annotations. The table is used to disseminate UoM information into a source program and detect errors at compile-time. The algorithm successfully exploits dimensional analysis rules for arithmetic operators within components [39]. This is an example of a static component based approach, and through this process of static UoM propagation checking, manages to perform a greater coverage than Damevski's run-time method.

A component based discipline means that the consequences of local unit mistakes are underestimated. The analysis of local assignment expressions will not occur in Damevski's scheme and will be limited in Ore's. On the other hand, checking at the component level allows diverse teams to collaborate even if their domain specific environments or choice of quantity systems were, to some extent, dissimilar. More importantly, either a static or dynamic component implementation would have been effective at correcting the Mars Climate Orbiter error.

4.4 Black-box testing

The last method that we will look at for checking quantities are managed correctly is known as black box automated testing. This method is usually applied to detect incorrect or missing methods, initialisation errors, interface errors and errors in data structures. By extrapolating use cases from the requirements specification to create unit tests, which are then systematically applied to the program, errors can be discovered before the code is put into operation. In the case of UoM tests, the resulting testing will not be comprehensive. Unit testing will focus on the correct initialisation of variables, the UoM correctness of assignments and method calls. This approach is also considered lightweight as no annotations are required in the program, however creating sufficient unit tests by hand is tedious. Efforts to generate unit tests from UML descriptions automatically [40–43], either through behavioural diagrams or with rule based approaches, are seen to be costly and non-trivial in practice [44].

Modern agile software development practices rely heavily on manually developing tests for enabling refactoring but also to support test driven development (TTD). Unit testing for UoM errors does not require any extra tool support, and will not alter any other parts of the system as shown in **Figure 6**, where we show the testing required for a simple UoM based addition function. If `t` is true then both arguments are in kilometres, alternatively the second argument is in miles and converted accordingly. The two test cases capture this intention. Many developers would argue that time spent becoming familiar with a UoM library, and updating their programs accordingly, might be better spend writing unit tests: *"I could use the same time to write tests and that would really find and prevent errors and at the same time not introduce a crazy complicated library every other developer in my team would have to deal with."* [28].

```
class Distance {
 public double add_km(boolean t,
                double a, double b) {
   return ((t)? a+b : a+(b*1.609));}}
...
public class DistanceTest {
 public void test_add_km() {
   Distance d = new Distance();
   assert(d.add_km(true,10.0,10.0)==20.0);
   assert(d.add_km(false,10.0,10.0)==26.09);}}
```

Figure 6.
Java code and JUnit test case for simple addition of two kilometres, or kilometre and mile distances [45].

However, the UoM knowledge will be localised to each particular unit so the slight implementation cost comes at the expense of potentially average checking.

5. Conclusions

Recent initiatives such as the FAIR data principles [46] emphasis machine-actionability of scientific data. With greater interoperability, industrial use of computational simulations and penetration of digitalisation through cyber-physical systems; there is an urgency to faithfully represent key properties of physical systems in code bases [1, 47].

We have endeavoured to provide the necessary background for software users to choose the most appropriate method for enabling quantity checking in code bases. Alas native language support is not available for popular programming languages. This situation is unlikely to change as it would require new language definitions and expensive compiler rewrites, with an important criteria of ensuring backwards compatibility with existing code. Validators solve some of these issues but require assurances that tool support will be maintained. DSL checkers are very effective for their given domain but lack generality. It is clear that even the best libraries currently cause significant performance issues while not being relevant for most developers. However some of the dynamic libraries include a lightweight syntax that makes UoM annotations significantly easier. A strength of component based techniques is that they can be undertaken at either compile-time or run-time with little overhead. They cede UoM checking completeness for a low annotation burden and ease of adoption. Approaches based on manual black-box testing frameworks offer many of the benefits of static component based techniques without requiring extra syntax. The drawback is that the UoM information will be implanted within the unit tests and not as a form of documentation within programs.

Annotating quantities in code bases is costly for developers [21] but relatively durable to software evolution. Refactoring does not change the external behaviour of the software, it will rarely require quantity annotation modifications unless there are changes to the core data structures. Techniques that manage UoM at compile-time, such as native language support or static lightweight solutions, allow unit conversions to be undertaken before code is created and values to be represented in unboxed form, thus resulting in better accuracy and efficiency.

The pros and cons of UoM techniques are listed in **Table 1** using features that are relevant to users. Native language or pluggable type based techniques offer many benefits, such as an equational UoM checker that is capable of resolving UoM type

Technique	Programming ease of use	Execution speed	Numeric accuracy	Ease of integration	Unit error detection
Native Support	High	Very High	Excellent	Low	Very High
Validator	High	High	Very Good	Average	Average
DSL	Low	High	Very Good	Low	Average
Static Library	Low	Average	Good	Low	High
Dynamic Library	Average	Low	Good	Low	High
Static Component	High	High	Very Good	High	Average
Dynamic Component	High	Average	Good	High	Low
Black Box Testing	Average	High	Very Good	Very High	Average

Table 1.
Contrasting alternative methods of implementing units of measurement in software projects, extended from [45].

variables, and unit conversion optimisation to improve run-time behaviour. Static component and black box based testing provide some of the benefits of static UoM libraries with less coverage but greater versatility. This is in tune with contemporary software development methods that favours lightweight techniques which integrate into existing digital platforms.

Software users who require a degree of robustness have had little say over how much validation was undertaken on their code to ensure UoM are handled correctly. This chapter aims to inform users and developers of the various options that exist to check that quantities are handled properly, along with the implications of these choices with regards to their software eco-system. The needs of a reactive and responsive on-line application, with assorted UoM input, are very different to a fully quantity specified stand-alone safety critical application. Nonetheless software-intensive systems are prevalent in our daily lives, with complex functionality and strong interconnection. The need to ensure quantity values behave correctly are greater than ever before.

Author details

Steve McKeever
Department of Informatics and Media, Uppsala University, Sweden

*Address all correspondence to: steve.mckeever@im.uu.se

References

[1] Hanisch R et al. Stop squandering data: Make units of measurement machine-readable. Nature. 2022;**605**: 222-224

[2] Arthur Stephenson, Lia LaPiana, Daniel Mulville, Frank Bauer Peter Rutledge, David Folta, Greg Dukeman, Robert Sackheim, and Peter Norvig. Mars Climate Orbiter Mishap Investigation Board Phase 1 Report, 1999. NASA Headquarters, Washington D.C., USA: NASA Press Release; [Last Accessed: May 19, 2022]

[3] James Clerk Maxwell. A Treatise on Electricity and Magnetism [Microform] / by James Clerk Maxwell. Oxford: Clarendon Press; 1873

[4] NIST. International System of Units (SI): Base and Derived. 2015. [Last Accessed: May 19, 2022]

[5] Karr M, Loveman DB. Incorporation of units into programming languages. Communications of the ACM. 1978; **21**(5):385-391

[6] Gehani N. Units of measure as a data attribute. Computer Languages. 1977; **2**(3):93-111

[7] Dreiheller A, Mohr B, Moerschbacher M. Programming pascal with physical units. SIGPLAN Notes. 1986;**21**(12):114-123

[8] Hilfinger PN. An Ada package for dimensional analysis. ACM Transactions on Programming Languages and Systems. 1988;**10**(2):189-203

[9] Fowler M. Analysis Patterns: Reusable Objects Models. Boston, MA, USA: Addison-Wesley Longman Publishing Co., Inc.; 1997

[10] McKeever S, Paçaci G, Bennich-Björkman O. Quantity checking through unit of measurement libraries, current status and future directions. In: Model-Driven Engineering and Software Development, MODELS WARD. Portugal: SciTePress; 2019

[11] Mayerhofer T, Wimmer M, Vallecillo A. Adding uncertainty and units to quantity types in software models. In: Software Language Engineering, SLE 2016. NY, USA: ACM; 2016. pp. 118-131

[12] Allen E, Chase D, Luchangco V, Maessen J-W, Steele GL Jr. Object-oriented units of measurement. In: Proceedings of Object-Oriented Programming, Systems, Languages, and Applications, OOPSLA '04. NY, USA: ACM; 2004. pp. 384-403

[13] McKeever S, Bennich-Björkman O, Salah O-A. Unit of measurement libraries, their popularity and suitability. Software: Practice and Experience. 2020; **51**(4):711-734

[14] Cooper J, McKeever S. A model-driven approach to automatic conversion of physical units. Software: Practice and Experience. 2008;**38**(4):337-359

[15] Antoniu T, Steckler PA, Krishnamurthi S, Neuwirth E, Felleisen M. Validating the unit correctness of spreadsheet programs. In: Proceedings of Software Engineering, ICSE '04. Washington, DC, USA: IEEE Computer Society; 2004. pp. 439-448

[16] Ore J-P, Detweiler C, Elbaum S. Lightweight detection of physical unit inconsistencies without program annotations. In: Proceedings of International Symposium on Software Testing and Analysis, ISSTA 2017. NY, USA: ACM; 2017. pp. 341-351

[17] Marcus Foster and Sean Tregeagle. Physical-Type Correctness in Scientific Python, CoRR, arXiv; 2018

[18] McKeever S. Discerning quantities from units of measurement. In: Proceedings of the 10th International Conference on Model-Driven Engineering and Software Development - MODELSWARD. Portugal: INSTICC, SciTePress; 2022. pp. 105-115

[19] Stevens SS. On the theory of scales of measurement. Science. 1946;**103**(2684): 677-680

[20] Hall B. The problem with 'dimensionless quantities'. In: Proceedings of the 10th International Conference on Model-Driven Engineering and Software Development - MODELSWARD. Portugal: INSTICC, SciTePress; 2022. pp. 116-125

[21] Ore J-P, Elbaum S, Detweiler C, Karkazis L. Assessing the type annotation burden. In: Automated Software Engineering, ASE 2018. NY, USA: ACM; 2018. pp. 190-201

[22] Wand M, O'Keefe P. Automatic dimensional inference. In: Computational Logic - Essays in Honor of Alan Robinson. Cambridge Massachusetts, USA: MIT Press; 1991. pp. 479-483

[23] Milner R. A theory of type polymorphism in programming. Journal of Computer and System Sciences. 1978; **17**:348-375

[24] Kennedy A. Dimension types. In: Sannella D, editor. Programming Languages and Systems—ESOP'94. Vol. 788. Edinburgh, U.K.: Springer; 1994. pp. 348-362

[25] TIOBE. The Importance of Being Earnest Index. 2022. Available from: https://www.tiobe.com/tiobe-index/ [Last Accessed: July 6]

[26] Apple. Swift open source. 2022. [Last Accessed: May 19, 2022]

[27] Microsoft. F# software foundation, 2020. [Last Accessed: May 19, 2022]

[28] Salah O-A, McKeever S. Lack of adoption of units of measurement libraries: Survey and anecdotes. In: Proceedings of Software Engineering in Practice, ICSE-SEIP '20. NY, USA: ACM; 2020

[29] Dieterichs Henning. Units of Measurement Validator for C#. [Last Accessed: May 19 2022]

[30] Jiang L, Zhendong S. Osprey: A practical type system for validating dimensional unit correctness of C programs. In: Proceedings of the 28th International Conference on Software Engineering, ICSE '06. New York, NY, USA: ACM; 2006. pp. 262-271

[31] Hills M, Feng C, Grigore R. A rewriting logic approach to static checking of units of measurement in C. Electronic Notes in Theoretical Computer Science. 2012;**290**:51-67

[32] Xiang T, Luo JY, Dietl W. Precise inference of expressive units of measurement types. Proceedings of the ACM on Programming Languages. 2020; **4**:1-28. (OOPSLA)

[33] Garny A, Nickerson D, Cooper J, dos Santos RW, Miller A, McKeever S, et al. Cellml and associated tools and techniques. Philosophical Transactions of the Royal Society, A: Mathematical, Physical and Engineering Sciences. 2008; **366**:3017-3043

[34] Bennich-Björkman O, McKeever S. The Next 700 Unit of Measurement Checkers. In Proceedings of Software Language Engineering, SLE 2018. NY,

USA: Association for Computing Machinery; 2018. pp. 121-132

[35] Bekolay T. A comprehensive look at representing physical quantities in python. Scientific Computing with Python. Proceedings of the 11th ACM SIGPLAN International Conference on Software Language Engineering. 2013. pp. 121-132

[36] Krisper M, Iber J, Rauter T, Kreiner C. Physical quantity: Towards a pattern language for quantities and units in physical calculations. In: Proceedings of Pattern Languages of Programs, EuroPLoP '17. NY, USA: ACM; 2017. p. 9:1–9:20

[37] Ore J-P, Elbaum S, Detweiler C. Dimensional inconsistencies in code and ROS messages: A study of 5.9m lines of code. In: 2017 IEEE/RSJ International Conference on Intelligent Robots and Systems (IROS). Manhattan, NY, USA: IEEE; 2017. pp. 712-718

[38] Damevski K. Expressing measurement units in interfaces for scientific component software. In: Proceedings of Component-Based High Performance Computing, CBHPC '09. NY, USA: ACM; 2009. p. 13:1–13:8

[39] Ore J-P, Detweiler C, Elbaum S. Phriky-units: A lightweight, annotation-free physical unit inconsistency detection tool. In: Software Testing and Analysis, ISSTA 2017. NY, USA: Association for Computing Machinery; 2017. pp. 352-355

[40] Alessandra Cavarra, Charles Crichton, Jim Davies, Alan Hartman, Thierry Jeron, and Laurent Mounier. Using UML for Automatic Test Generation. Proceedings of ISSTA. NY, USA: ACM SIGSOFT International Symposium on Software Testing and Analysis; 2002

[41] Hartmann J, Vieira M, Foster H, Ruder A. A UML-based approach to system testing. Innovations in Systems and Software Engineering. 2005;**1**:12-24

[42] Ali S, Hemmati H, Holt NE, Arisholm E, Briand LC. Model transformations as a strategy to automate model-based testing-a tool and industrial case studies. In: Simula Research Laboratory, Technical Report (2010-01). Norway: Technical Report, Simula Research Laboratory and University of Oslo; 2010. pp. 1-28

[43] Mussa M, Ouchani S, Sammane W, Hamou-Lhadj A. A Survey of Model-Driven Testing Techniques. Proceedings - International Conference on Quality Software. QSIC. 2009. Manhattan, NY, USA: IEEE; pp. 167-172

[44] Kasurinen J, Taipale O, Smolander K. Software test automation in practice: Empirical observations. Advances in Software Engineering. 2010;**2010**:01

[45] McKeever S. From quantities in software models to implementation. In: Proceedings of the 9th International Conference on Model-Driven Engineering and Software Development - MODELSWARD. Portugal: INSTICC, SciTePres; 2021. pp. 199-206

[46] Wilkinson MD, Dumontier M, Aalbersberg IJJ, Appleton G, Axton M, Baak A, et al. The fair guiding principles for scientific data management and stewardship. Scientific Data. 2016;**3**:1-9

[47] Selic B. Beyond mere logic: A vision of modeling languages for the 21st century. In: Pervasive and Embedded Computing and Communication Systems (PECCS). Portugal: SciTePress; 2015. p. IS09

Section 3

Testing for Usability

Chapter 4

Usability Testing Methods and Usability Laboratory Management

Josef Pavlíček and Petra Pavlíčková

Abstract

Usability testing of software products is of key importance nowadays. In order for usability testing to have the desired effect, the appropriate testing methodology must be chosen. Usability testing can be carried out using qualitative or quantitative methods. A widely used qualitative method today is the heuristic evaluation proposed by Jacob Nielsen. However, there are other testing methods such as cognitive walkthrough or collaborative testing (proposed by Josef Pavlicek and R. Bock). Although heuristic analysis has generally received a lot of attention in the current literature, it is important to put the other methods in the right light. These provide a significantly better view of the user's passage through the interface under test. The methods better simulate the environment in which the final UI will operate. The user experience (UX) is then significantly better measurable if the participant goes through the test scenario in a cognitive (i.e., mental model-defined) way, rather than by mere heuristic evaluation. A significant milestone is then the cognitive-collaborative passage, where the collaborative element of the evaluators contributes to the evaluation of the solution.

Keywords: use case, scenario, Persona, user group, usability, usability testing, usability scenario, heuristic evaluation, cognitive walkthrough, collaborative walkthrough, UI Lab, collaborative UI Lab, testing, remote testing, qualitative and quantitative usability study

1. Introduction

Creating user-friendly user interfaces is a hot topic at the moment. A quality user interface is easy to use, looks attractive, and gives the user a good user experience. This experience is called user experience, hence the abbreviation UX [1]. In order to design a good user interface, it is necessary to understand the user [1, 2]. The next step is to be able to use technology to best implement the requirements. The other step is to be able to test the user interface. The overall test is called a usability test and is subject to a number of rules. They need to be learned. It should be understood how to learn this knowledge. If these factors of knowledge and skills are combined, results can be expected to go beyond user-friendliness to achieve excellent results. And that is the art of user interface design. This chapter covers the methodology and practices one should adopt, to become a proficient eXperience designer. And just like with mixing cocktails, on the one hand, you need to follow the tried and true procedures (a cookbook) [3, 4], so too is your inventiveness, training, and experience, which you will only achieve with honest practice. The focus of our contribution is to teach readers how to practice interaction design methods.

The design of user interfaces is thematically divided into the following chapters:

User Definition: In this section, authors explain the mental model of the user. Using examples, the authors show the reader how the mental model is affected. They give illustrative examples of how the mental model is affected. They show its influence on the user's decision-making. The authors describe how a user interface should behave in order to have a positive influence on the user's mental model.

Persona and User Groups: In this section, the authors explain which tools can be used to get a good understanding of user behavior. In the previous section, the mental model of the user was explained. Now, it is necessary to explain how a user with the desired mental model can be found or, rather, how to understand the mental model of a potential user. To do this, the archetypes of Persona user models or Focus Groups users will be used.

Usability: In this section, the authors explain possible methods for testing the user interface. UI testing is a challenging discipline and deserves its own chapter in the book. Therefore, they limit themselves to the most important aspects of user interface testing. They describe heuristic analysis and cognitive walkthrough. They show other testing methods and their advantages.

2. User definition

First, let's define the user. Who is a user? It is the person who uses our app and is willing to pay for it. And because interaction designers strive to do great work and service, they want to get paid well for it. So, they need to know how the prospective user responds and what their needs are. In other words, you need to know the mental model of the user (**Figure 1**).

2.1 Mental model

A mental model is an explanation of someone's thought process about how something works in the real world. It is a representation of the surrounding world, the relationships between its various parts and a person's intuitive perception about his or

Figure 1.
Who is the user?.

her own acts, and their consequences. Mental models can help shape behavior and set an approach to solving problems (similar to a personal algorithm) and doing tasks.

Jay Wright Forrester [4] defined general mental models as: "*The image of the world around us, which we carry in our head, is just a model. Nobody in his head imagines all the world, government or country. He has only selected concepts, and relationships between them, and uses those to represent the real system*"

For the user-centered design (UCD), it will be useful to leave psychological theory behind and to be more practical.

User mental model from the UCD point of view:

- Human adaptation to use machine according to gained experience.
- Shapes human perception of using machine.
- If anything is broken, user feels wrong and does not want to use the machine.
- Depends on age and gender (children are more adaptive than adults).
- Is influenced by geographical conditions.
- Is influenced by nationality.
  - Perception of symbols (typical example).
  - Swastika (European symbol of war. In Hinduism, the swastika is considered an exceptionally holy and positive symbol and is therefore very often used on all occasions).
  - Crucifix (Christian symbol of human savior, for Romans, a method of capital punishment).

The mental model is best modeled with the help of the so-called Persona; see section Persona.

2.1.1 Manifestation of the mental model

- It shapes human perception toward understanding and using the user interface.
- Depends on age and gender (children and young people are logically the most adaptive).
- Manifested, for example, in the perception of colors and symbols (there is a strong cultural influence here—typically the perception of swastika symbols).
- If violated, the user feels uncomfortable and stupid and refuses to use the machine (this state is to be avoided).

2.1.2 Emotions and the mental model

The mental model manifests itself in the emotions of the user (**Table 1**).

Now, the reader should learn how each emotion affects the user and how it affects their evaluation of the user experience.

Emotions are generally divided into							
Fear	Anger	Joy	Sadness	Confidence	Disgust	Expectations	Surprise

Table 1.
Human beings' emotions.

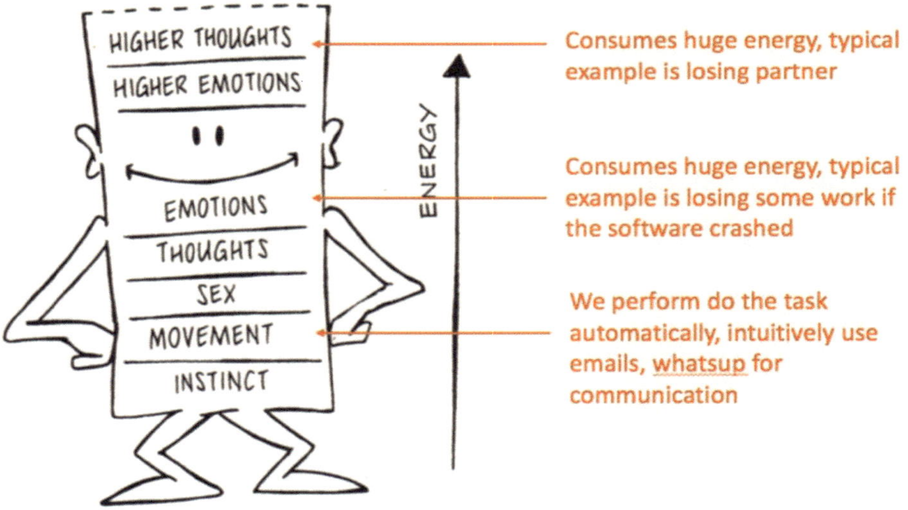

Figure 2.
Mental model schema.

In general, interaction design or user-centered design (UCD) distinguishes between low emotional load and high emotional load (**Figure 2**).

2.1.3 Low emotional load

It is typical in that although it affects us negatively (creates a negative feeling of fear, anger, surprise) it is manageable and, depending on the type of software product, acceptable. A sample of such load is "unnecessary large number of clicks," placing various controls in unexpected places. This load can be eliminated by learning how to work with the application and is tolerated in applications that are complex and technologically advanced in their foundation: graphic editors, CAD systems, etc. It is unavoidable for complex software products. Computer technological capabilities, and legal and safety regulations can significantly affect them.

This kind of load should not occur with leisure equipment. However, the rule of system complexity also applies here. Take the example of Tetris. The controls should be intuitive. Contrary to a transport aircraft simulator, here the controls will be less intuitive. The controls will therefore impose a certain mental load. However, this will be accepted by the player. After all, controlling an aircraft is challenging

2.1.4 High emotional load

This kind of load must not appear in our solutions. It is a load that brings the user into severe emotional states such as loss of confidence, disgust, and anger. It appears whenever the software performs an operation that is emotionally arousing.

DOI: http://dx.doi.org/10.5772/intechopen.109140

For example:

- It does not save work in progress.
- The printout is not formatted correctly, even though the preview is correct.
- The work is unexpectedly terminated or, on the contrary, the task cannot be completed (such a pattern is, e.g., the former behavior of Windows updates, when trying to shut down the computer, the computer does not continue its shutdown task and updates the computer for another 15 minutes ... the user in the meantime urgently needs to catch the train taking him home from work).
- Computer crash, etc.

2.2 How emotions affect SW evaluation

For the purpose of UX, it is enough to remember that the user load caused by **repetitive routines is acceptable** to some extent.

Stresses affecting the user's feelings (anger caused by the loss of important data and work ... e.g., unsaved chapters in a master's thesis, etc.) is deeply imprinted in the user's memory. The latter then intuitively discriminates the solution, even if the bug is already fixed in the next version.

2.3 Rules of UI behavior toward the user

2.3.1 Be goal (UseCases) oriented

Remember that every user goal (UseCase) that is implemented in the form of buttons, screens, and other components should be implemented as simply as possible and with a minimum of energy. This is the direction in which the UX rules defined by Jacob Nielsen lead; see the Usability chapter.

2.3.2 The machine should always help

In general, it should be understood that the purpose of a machine or computer program is always to help the human (user). If it stops helping and starts harming, it becomes a hated monster. It is important how the machine alerts the human to a critical condition. The relevant dialog was not meant to be hidden.

2.3.3 Don't make a fool of me!

From the original "Don't Make Me Feel Stupid!" It tries to suggest to designers that good software will guide and help the user. It will not confront them with frustrating tasks and ask them inappropriate questions (**Figure 3**).

2.3.4 Don't stress the user with unnecessary questions

Recognize that software is supposed to help the user. It is supposed to anticipate his actions, automatically assuming that the data loss is fatal (i.e., no need to ask

Figure 3.
A confused user feels uncomfortable!.

whether to actually save). Only when there is a real danger of data corruption by the user's decision, to warn him.

2.3.5 Inform me clearly about errors

Error messages are essential in UI and are very often underestimated by designers. It is important to remember that the user is not the programmer. He is not even an analyst and did not design the application. What is obvious to us as developers, for example, a connection to the database crashed, is incomprehensible to the average user. Therefore, messages like in **Table 2**.

Each message must be translated into the user's language, and others cannot appear in the UI. Thus, for example:

- MyTextEdit could not save the last edit. Check that you seem to have enough disk space and repeat the save operation. If the failure persists, save the work to an external disk and contact the administrator.

However, never forget Hick's law, which says [5–8]: "*The reaction time required for the user to complete his task therefore increases with the number of available options.*" Simply put, the more objects in front of the user, the longer it takes to make a selection.

Wrong error messages example
The program has performed an invalid operation and will be terminated.
An overflow has occurred at address A3453BCH122AA.
ORA-00933: SQL command not properly ended.

Table 2.
Error message example.

2.3.6 The principle of avoiding surprises

The average computer user likes not to be surprised by anything. Some parts of the user interface should stay in the same place and not change significantly. A typical example is the user menu. If images or icons are used, they should always have the same expression throughout the user's passage through the program. The user is unnecessarily surprised and confused if the meaning of the icons changes. In that case, he stops liking the program he is using and runs the risk of becoming frustrated with it. Such a case leads to abandoning the program and replacing it with another more intuitive one.

2.3.7 Restrictions on the use of icons

Let's remember that the icon is closely related to the mental model of the user. Under the pictogram (i.e., icon), different users can easily imagine different meanings. Therefore, the use of icons in the user interface should be minimized. They should be placed where the operation is often repeated. On the other hand, operations that do not occur frequently should rather be supplemented with a textual description, hence the following rule of thumb for navigating the user interface using navigation elements:

1. **Textual description** (absolutely clear).

2. **Icon with text description** (nice design, unfortunately, duplicates the description and graphic meaning).

3. **Text bubble help icon** (ideal for frequently repeated operations, but has less telling power than a text description).

4. **Icon without description and bubble help** (used only for chronically known operations inherited from the operating system = minimize, maximize, move, close = window edge operations).

5. **Graphical symbols** (buttons, sliders, etc., no longer belong to the primary communication elements and are covered by the Interaction Design dimensions).

In this section, let us cite five basic principles of human-PC interaction called the five dimensions of Interaction Design. The concept of dimensions of interaction design was introduced in Moggridge's book Designing Interactions [9]. Gillan Crampton Smith [10] wrote that interaction design draws on four existing design languages, 1D, 2D, 3D, 4D. Kevin Silver later proposed a fifth dimension, behavior [11]. Let us quote Josef Pavlicek [3] and Kevin Silver [11]:

> ***Words:*** *This dimension defines interactions: words are the element that users interact with.*
> ***Visual representations:*** *Visual representations are the elements of an interface that the user perceives; these may include but are not limited to "typography, diagrams, icons, and other graphics".*
> ***Physical objects or space:*** *This dimension defines the objects or space "with which or within which users interact".*

> ***Time:*** *The time during which the user interacts with the interface. An example of this includes "content that changes over time such as sound, video or animation".*
> ***Behavior:*** *Behavior defines how users respond to the interface. Users may have different reactions in this interface.*

2.3.8 The limitations of human memory

To make the use of a computer pleasant and ergonomic for the user, it is necessary not to rely on its memory. In addition, other important features must also be considered. Referring to the book by J. Pavlíček [3], **Table 3** can be briefly explained as common rules.

2.4 System feedback

As you go through the software, you need to communicate to the user what is happening or what has just happened. If the user does not know or is not clear, he or she will most likely stop using the software.

The most basic physical feedback is very important. For example, when a user types "help," the word "help" should appear on the screen. Physical feedback includes all kinds of feedback, from system sounds to the sound of a mouse click to actually highlighting text if the user clicks on it and hovers the mouse over it, for example.

If there is an operation going on in the program that requires waiting, the user should also be informed of this. For example, an hourglass or a window with the progress of the operation (Progress bar) is established.

You should **remember**: The user interface should respond to every user action.

If the user moves the mouse, the mouse cursor must move. The guidelines for your chosen operating system (e.g., MacOS Human Interface Guidelines) describe the basic behavior of the user interface. These should be kept in mind by every application developer. They should be followed by the software development. The basic rules include **response time** (**Table 4**):

Care should be taken: There are several variations of status bars. Usually for an operation where the duration can be calculated (either you know the processing speed or you know the number of operations to be performed), it is advisable to use a percentage = incremental status line. Such a case is, for example, performing a search for a text string in files on disk. If the total number of required operations is known, it

The common rule	System behavior
Important information	Alerts, warnings—should not disappear from the screen after a short time!
Data fields should be arranged	In the order the user expects them, or as is usual on similar sites. Required fields should be in sequence, not in skip order with optional ones.
Make the user's job easier	You can help, for example, by automatically formatting the phone number "+1-250-0197-2500" instead of "+125001972500."
Provide help and information	Inform about where the user is, or how they got there.
If something is wrong, inform	Inform the user with ongoing feedback. For example, breadcrumb help.

Table 3.
How to help the user.

is easy to calculate what percentage of the work has already been done by the machine and display this information on the screen. If it is not possible to predict the processing time (or it is not possible to show the user what percentage of the total has already been processed—the processing time is likely to vary according to the performance of the user's machine), then an infinite status bar is used. This moves from right to left. This signals the user that the operation is still being executed. A typical case might be loading a file of unknown length from the Internet (but it is recommended to avoid this feature if possible).

2.4.1 User attention

Techniques for gaining user attention need to be handled very carefully, especially when designing software. Various flashing banners and pop-ups are usually distracting. The same goes for very rich colors. Users tend to ignore overly significant elements, and the so-called Banner Blindness phenomenon arises. Too strong elements are ignored by users as if they were ads.

It is also advisable not to use more than four different font sizes on one page and a maximum of three different fonts, and it is also not advisable to write only in capital letters. Use text underlining and highlighting only rarely.

NOTE: Underlining the letters in a word is a very useful UI element. The so-called mnemonic aids help to use shortcuts for various operations, see: CTRL + S = Save ... Unfortunately, these aids disappear from new operating systems. However, orientation-intensive tools, where the user is expected to adapt deeply to the machine and use abbreviations, still use them.

2.4.2 First-Time experience

This rule (confirmed by J.Pavlíček, R. Bock during the UI Studies) says that there is a very close correlation between how the solution is given to the user (in our case primarily software, but it can also be HW and SW = mobile phone) acts during the first hour. If the user is still not safe in the basic user goals after the first hour of using the solution, then his willingness to use it decreases. This is a very dangerous condition. It affects all software solutions that are not highly specialized for a given activity and are in fact a trend issue: be it Open-Source SW, operating system, and mobile phone programs, after the personal computer operating system.

2.4.3 Houmer Simpson Car issue

The user interface must meet a perfectly limited area of requirements. Respectively, it must be specialized for primary persons. The success of the overall solution is

Response time	**Behavior**
Less than 3 seconds	The UI does not perform any informational activity.
Longer than 3 seconds and shorter than 20 seconds	UI displays an hourglass or an icon symbolizing waiting.
Longer than 20 seconds	UI displays a status bar (progress bar)

Table 4.
Response time behavior.

based on the definition of person. This is very important to realize if the people are poorly designed, then the overall UI/UX will also be bad. If properly designed, then the UI must best meet the requirements of the primary person. The requirements of Persona B must allow, but it does not matter that there will be any mental burden on the user. The requirements of a negative C person should not meet, but can only perform as a secondary effect of other functionalities (**Figure 4**).

It is not possible to satisfy everyone's requirements equally. It is never possible to satisfy the requirements of all users. This is something to keep in mind. It is a common mistake of beginner designers. This mistake is now in UX slang by "Houmer Simpson's car." It satisfies a wide range of average users but always only partially. After all, it is not suitable for "cottages" or "shopping." The desire to satisfy everyone is very strong, and this mistake manifests itself very often. Just look at the experiments of, for example, car factories with some cars. Certainly, similar diameters can be found in world brands. So, watch out for that.

3. Persona and user groups

In order to understand how to properly design a user interface, it is necessary to model the future user. Then focus the user design specifically on their needs. Of course, this depends closely on the type of product being developed and the means available to present it to the public. If the designer is innovative enough (like Steve Jobs with smartphones, for example), then he does not need a model user. He creates the product and markets it through advertising and technological presentation. However, this is both very risky and very expensive. So if he is developing a more or less traditional software product, then he should follow the established principles (be more careful with innovation). With the help of model users, say whether such a user exists in real life (because he wants to sell the solution). If so, he will use it for the design. Here it is all about Personas.

Figure 4.
Homer Simpson car issue [12].

DOI: http://dx.doi.org/10.5772/intechopen.109140

3.1 Persona

Personas are archetypes that describe the various goals and observed behavior patterns among users. A persona encapsulates critical behavioral data in a way that both designers and stakeholders can understand, remember, and relate to.

Personas use storytelling to engage users' social and emotional aspects, which helps designers to either visualize the best product behavior or see why the recommended design is successful.

A persona is a fictional character, which is used while designing an application, website, or technology. The persona represents a fictional user of the tested application, which has its own personality, needs, characteristics, specific approaches, and opinions:

- It is created from the data collected during user interviews or with the use of some other statistical methods.
- Personas are created by implementing common behavioral patterns of more users into one fictional person.
- Using personas in creating projects puts a human face to otherwise abstract data and allows the designers to easily understand the needs of the fictional characters.

3.2 Persona variants

The authors suggest to recognizing three types of personas:

Persona A: A is a typical user. (S)he will use all functionalities, and the system MUST BE implemented for him/her. It is necessary to design GUIs for that person's business goals-derive UseCases from them! (**Figure 5**)

Figure 5.
Persona A can be young girl.

Figure 6.
Persona B can be a boy.

Persona B: B is an occasional user. The GUI is not primarily implemented for this user. But the GUI should address his UseCases. However, these UseCases can be time- and energy-consuming. Although he/she is not the primary user of the system, we need to provide him/her with some ways to complete his/her business goals (UseCases) (**Figure 6**).

Persona C: C is a negative persona. It is sometimes called antipersona. This user NEVER uses the system.

In general, different kinds of model users can be created. However, the authors recommend only the following three types. The authors consider the other variants to be redundant. The user interface should be designed for the primary personas! Other personas are users who do not primarily use the system. However, they should be able to work with the system. A negative persona is a user who will NEVER use the system. It is introduced for contrast or because of a different view of UI functionality that should NOT be part of it. It is a view that should be avoided (**Figures** 7 and **8**).

3.3 User group

In some cases, the definition of Personas is somewhat complicated. Or it is not suitable because a large number of model personas would need to be created. In this case, it is appropriate to define the group as Persona. These are typically information site designs. Such sites where there are a large number of user groups. A clear (and painfully tested) example is the university website. Many requirements are mixed here, and it is very difficult to decide who is actually the primary person.

Universities must always address:

Figure 7.
Persona C never uses the system.

Persona A

- **Name**: Arthur Dent
- **Age** – 35
- **Gender** – Male
- **Hobbies** – Children's toys, carving puppets, children's rooms design
- **Typical day** – Arthur gets up at 7 o'clock and has a quick breakfast - Croissant and coffee. Then he rides a bicycle or if it is raining by bus to work downtown. He dresses sporty. As a designer of children's rooms, they often walk around clients' apartments. That's why he prefers sportswear and shoes. He prefers to use a pencil, notebook, folding ruler. In the evening, goes to the center for a beer with friends, or to the puppet theater of the local association.
- **Short history** – Arthur is kind, helpful, and somewhat cautiously withdrawn; he is constantly on the lookout for his mouth and tries not to cause any trouble; that is why he likes mundaneness and quite boring. After graduating from elementary school, he went to a construction industrial school. He graduated. Now he works as a residential architect and prefers to design children's rooms or houses, built so that children can live well in them. Switches and handles low, soft carpets and decorative wooden toys are typical of his artistic expression. His last, somewhat eccentric act was the hitchhiking of a Vogon construction ship with his friend, Ford Perfect.

Figure 8.
Persona A example form.

- Students (young people, doctoral and postdoctoral applicants, students of the University of the Third Age).
- Teachers, professional assistants, other roles such as accountants, PR.
- Parents and sponsors.
- State apparatus and bureaucracy.
- Industry, services, art.
- Other schools.

Defining a persona can be challenging. Therefore, it is possible to create user groups and label them as people on A, B, and C.

Authors personally do not recommend this method. Our practice is to make it safer to create honest people. Personas can possibly be assigned to groups of the type (teacher, student, and parent).

4. Usability

The term Usability is defined [13] by the international standardization organization ISO (ISO / TR 16982: 2002 standard) as authors quote: [14] ISO/TR 16982:2002 ("Ergonomics of human-system interaction—Usability methods supporting human-centered design") is an International Standards Organization (ISO) standard that provides information on human-centered usability methods that can be used for design and evaluation. It details the advantages, disadvantages, and other factors relevant to using each usability method. It explains the implications of the stage of the life cycle and the individual project characteristics for the selection of usability methods and provides examples of usability methods in context.

Applicability is also defined by Jakob Nielsen (whose principles are based here) [1, 2]. The usability attributes are visible at the **Table 5**.

The above attributes are necessary in order to measure user friendliness.

4.1 UseCase and scenarios

4.1.1 UseCase

In software and systems engineering, a use case is a list of actions or event steps typically defining the interactions between a role (known in the Unified Modeling Language (UML) as an actor) and a system to achieve a goal. The actor can be a human or other external system. In systems engineering, use cases are used at a higher level than within software engineering, often representing missions or stakeholder goals. The detailed requirements may then be captured in the Systems Modeling Language (SysML) or as contractual statements.

Use case analysis is an important and valuable requirement analysis technique that has been widely used in modern software engineering since its formal introduction by

The Nilesen's usability attributes	
Attribute name	**Explanation**
Simplicity of learning to use the system:	To learn to use a similar system faster.
Recall:	To remember the way from one situation to another
Efficiency:	To carry out the task quickly and efficiently
Minimum amount of errors:	If encountered, inform the users on the cause and an advice how to proceed
Satisfaction of the user:	The users is convinced that the task has been successfully achieved

Table 5.
Nielsen usability attributes.

Ivar Jacobson in 1992 [15]. Use case-driven development is a key characteristic of many process models and frameworks such as ICONIX, the Unified Process (UP), the IBM Rational Unified Process (RUP), and the Oracle Unified Method (OUM). With its inherent iterative, incremental, and evolutionary nature, use case also fits well for agile development.

The creation of UseCases has evolved, and a number of derivations have emerged since the so-called fully dressed UseCases. There is no space in this chapter to deal with the development of UseCases. Therefore, let us skip straight to the method that has worked well for us in designing UseCases.

UseCases are always based on the goals (user requirements) of the software. It goes without saying that one requirement can be implemented by a different number of UseCases. Therefore, the following rule should always be kept in mind:

A UseCase is a user's business goal, which he wants to achieve as quickly as possible for the least amount of effort expended.

UseCase should always be written from the **user's point of view**. It is written from the perspective of the **user's expectations!**

It is necessary to distinguish between the user's **expectation** and the **demand**.

The difference between the two words is crucial and should be in the ratio of 80 (expected) : 20 (required) in UCD and UX documents.

This is because UseCases are created (written) at a time when the form of the application is unknown (or mostly unknown). It lacks its controls, which must be derived from UseCases. If a button was required for every desired user action already in the UseCase (e.g., printing a report), then it may be that the controls are designed differently in 1000 UseCases.

There is a risk that each software analyst and designer who creates them may have a different idea of the final implementation of the operation. Consequently, identical operations will differ in implementation. This is another common mistake due to improperly created UseCases.

After all, this is common today. Different parts of the applications have different controls (although they are in accordance with the prescribed Look and Feel of the operating system). Usually, a huge mental burden is put on the programmer in the end, because he then has to implement it.

UseCase is therefore written in terms of user expectations, and it is necessary to avoid defining graphical controls.

For example: the user **expects** to enter the name of the print report and the number of pages, and sets the printer type. The user confirms the request (**it doesn't say how or by what!**).

Only if the user is forced to define a control for some important reason (is limited by health-color blindness, for example), then should be used the word **demand**.

4.1.2 Scenario

The opposite side of UseCases is the scenario. This is always written from the point of view of the system and how the system satisfies the user's requirements. So in this example, the system will display a print report icon, a text box to enter the number of pages, a combo button to select the printer, and a print button.

The scenario is always precise and describes the controls of the system. It is usually written after UseCase is finished, and there exist prototypes of the screens in the form of wireframes.

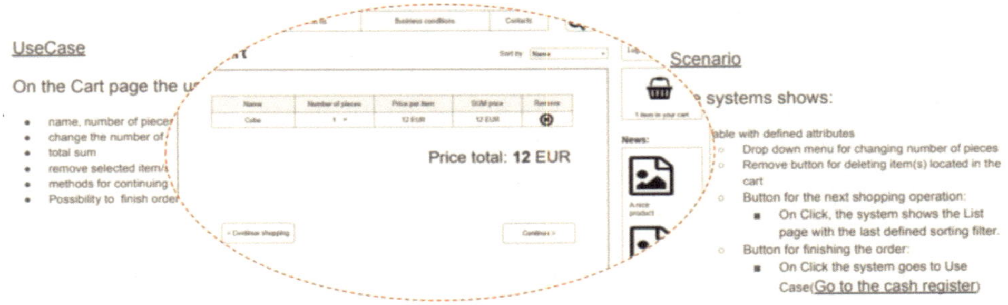

Figure 9.
UseCase, WireFrame, Scenario example.

4.1.3 UseCase and scenario in UCD

Therefore, the post of writing UseCase and Scenario is generally as follows:

- First, write UseCase in terms of user expectations. Avoid defining controls. Remember, it's too early for that.
- Design a wired screen model for one or more pooled user targets—UseCase.
- According to expectations and wire models, implement the scenario. This will match the look and feel of the application and describe how the system satisfies the user's expectations (**Figure 9**).

4.2 Usability testing

Usability testing is key to understanding and evaluating the quality of the designed user interface:

- **The aim is to improve** or update an application.
  - Should answer the question how and what to update.
- **Measuring how** human-made **products meet** its intended **purpose.**
- **Observe** people (personas) **using the product** to discover errors and areas of improvement.
- **Verifying** that real **users can use the system:**
  - Understanding how the real users (will) interact with the system.
  - Identification of problems that prevent real users from using the system.

The testing procedure is as follows:
Define the usability test framework:

- Define which parties participate in the test (client, developer, user, and sample).

- Define what is the purpose of testing, for whom is it intended, and what hypotheses is confirmed or refuted.
- Define on which technology the test will be performed:
    - Above the prototype.
    - Above the existing solution.
- Define where it will be executed:
    - On site.
    - UI lab.
    - Remote.
- Decide on the testing method:
    - **Without users**—expert review:
        1. Heuristic evaluation.
        2. Cognitive walkthrough.
        3. Collaborative walkthrough.
    - **With users:**
        1. User surveys.
        2. Ethnographic observations.
        3. Usability engineering.
        4. Collaborative usability engineering [16, 17].
- Variants of usability testing methods:
    - Qualitative.
    - Quantitative.
- Define a story that explains the reason for testing.
- Define a time frame.

4.2.1 Participants' definitions

Study participants should be primarily sponsors and stakeholders. Furthermore, creators who learn from their mistakes. Last but not least, application designers, software analysts, and testers should be represented.

4.2.2 Testing purpose

It is important to know the purpose of the test. The test can be done because of a negative "First-Time Experience." Or, on the other hand, a new system has been created and needs to be tested. It is also possible to test only the design. The design can take the form of paper prototypes, Lo-Fi or Hi-Fi prototypes. The following questions should always be asked as in **Table 6**.

4.2.3 Testing technology

Various tools can be used for testing. The most common are prototypes. These can be divided into two groups:

Lo-Fi prototype: This prototype requires a relatively short lead time. In the order of hours (paper prototype and pencil sketches) or days (clickable tools in Case, such as FIGMA). It is possible to create a large number of prototype variants. This prototype does not address the final look. Colors and color schemes can be designed as sketches. The prototype does not communicate with the core of the application, and there are no technology links.

Hi-Fi Prototype: This prototype is time- and money-consuming. It simulates the appearance of the future application. It often runs on the final platform. Look and Feel is defined and represents the final look and feel. Very often it is part of the implementation (clickable UI without connection to the core system).

Finished application: The last option is an already finished application. This testing method is very efficient for agile sw development methods. It will be used when the developer can communicate with the client. Testing is done in short iterations. Fixes are fast. Large software products can be developed in this way (if the developer follows the rules of agile development). It is also generally used when fixing a finished application.

4.2.4 Testing environment

The environment in which the testing takes place is equally crucial. In general, they can be divided into environments.

On Site: that is, in the user's office or wherever the application is to be used. The advantage is that there are natural and therefore realistic conditions. The user uses learned technologies and environments to control the application. Confusions such as "I have a different mouse," and "The chair is not comfortable" can be avoided.

The disadvantage is that conditions may vary according to different offices. This makes it difficult to repeat tests. It is also very difficult to use the company's offices for the tests. In an open-space office, other tasks than usability testing are generally performed. The work tasks of non-participating employees can disturb the progress of the test, and even *vice versa*, the test can be disturbing for non-participants.

This method is suitable for small projects or projects run according to agile methodologies.

What and how will we test		
What is the test goal?	What is new in the test?	What the test is not?

Table 6.
Test questions.

UI Lab: The specialized environment for usability testing is called UI Labs. Currently, there are several types of these labs. There is probably no general classification of them at the moment. Therefore, let us divide them here. In authors' experience, it seems to be an appropriate method to divide UI Labs according to the type of studies we perform. These studies (authors discuss them in more detail below) can be carried out with a focus on:

- Participants: This is generally heuristic analysis and cognitive walkthrough
- On collaboration: Cognitive walkthrough and collaborative walkthrough [14, 16, 17]

4.3 Participant-oriented UI Lab

If the UI Lab is participant-oriented, then its architecture is subordinate to that.

The room in which the participant performs the usability test has one or two workstations. This room is generally separated from the observer room by a one-way transparent mirror. This is transparent from the observer room so that they can observe the progress of the usability test. This is where the UI observers are in the front row to record the progress of the test. Next are the programmers and application stakeholders.

This UI Lab is significantly oriented toward the individual (participant) by its architecture. The testing method is then predominantly Jacob Nilsen = Heuristic. Sometimes the cognitive walkthrough method is performed (**Figure 10**).

However, from our experience [14, 16, 17], there is a criticism of this solution as in **Table** 7.

4.4 Collaboration-oriented UI Lab

I created this kind of UI Lab with Rudolf Bock as part of a research project at the Faculty of Management and Economics of the Czech University of Life Sciences [19, 20]. Authors call it Collaborative UI Lab. This kind of lab (covered by a national

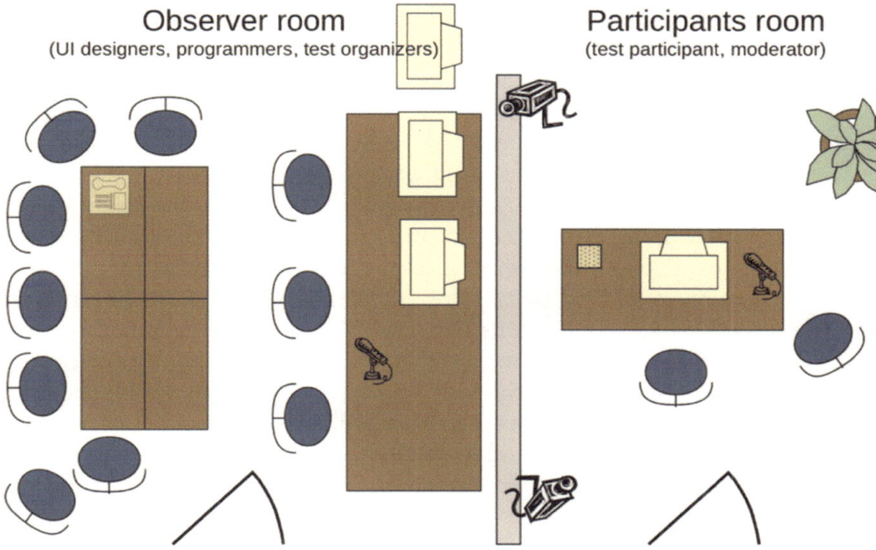

Figure 10.
Participant-oriented UI Lab [18].

Advantages	Disadvantages
Recorded results are well presented and well processed.	The environment is not real. Nowadays, when it is common to connect with colleagues *via* social networks and work in Open Space offices, it is not common for a user to be alone when working with SW.
It is well known what kind of work the participant is doing.	A participant sitting alone (or connected to the test moderator) and aware of his/her observations, probably puts more effort to find a way through the system. In this case, the test is burdened by mental error. Often self-doubt about one's own abilities will prevent the participant from passing a true assessment of the UI elements. This partially limits the thinking-at-the-voice rule.
Thinking aloud means the mental activity of the participant.	There is no real-time testing of processes (i.e., not only UI but also usability of work processes).

Table 7.
UI Lab benefits.

utility patent – PUV 2016-32993) actually responds to the shortcomings of the original architecture. It allows for extensive real-time testing of processes. At the same time, it allows to perform classical Usability testing. It also allows pair testing or interacting (collaborative) testing. This is the innovative approach promoted by see [14, 16, 17].

The collaborative testing lab contains two essentially semicircular tables, each containing at least three workstations, each station containing a computer, a monitor with a camera to capture the user's face, headphones and microphone, and a means for audio recording, with the tables positioned so that the center of the imaginary circle of which the table is a part faces the other table, and furthermore, the axes of symmetry of the two tables are parallel and offset from each other (i.e., and not identical), and the workstation monitors are positioned on each table such that the screens are positioned away from the other table. The central workstation of each table is equipped with means for tracking eye movements. The laboratory shall further comprise at least four wide-angle cameras, at least two of which shall be positioned to image the workstations including the monitor screens. In addition, the laboratory shall contain at least two loudspeakers.

In a preferred embodiment, each semicircular table comprises at least five workstations.

The speakers may preferably comprise a fixed or detachable video camera.

The laboratory may preferably be equipped with control means for the wide-angle cameras, means for converting the video signal to a digital signal, and means for recording and editing images transmitted by the cameras or sound from the microphones.

The individual elements may be connected by wires or wirelessly.

According to the presented technical solution, the laboratory allows several test participants to solve one task at the same time. Each of them can perform and be recorded as an individual and/or as a member of a team. This makes it possible to include the influence of social ties in the team in the testing and thus to make the testing closer to reality. Models focusing on team behavior can also be tested in this way. Because participants are tested under exactly the same conditions, the predictive value and statistical evaluation is easier and more relevant.

The semicircular shape of the tables and the placement of the monitors on them ensure that the individual users are not dependent, but the monitors can still be rotated so that 2–3 participants can work together if this is appropriate for the proposed test. The semicircular shape of the tables further creates a sense of unity and coherence of the working group and also ensures equal working conditions for the participants (**Figure 11**).

The layout of the lab allows for the placement of the test participants so that their faces and their gazes are directed to the space between the tables where the facilitator/testing guide can stand. At the same time, no one has to stand behind the participants, so they do not feel they are looking over their shoulders.

The study facilitator has the option of communicating with study participants individually through headphones or with all of them simultaneously (and identically) through speakers.

In one convenient embodiment, the lab is further equipped with a removable screen placed between the two tables. Screens can advantageously be placed on either side of the screen. The screen allows for competitive tests to be conducted, and brings the possibility of measuring behavior within the competitive environment and its effect on the solution of the task.

Depending on the technical design, the lab is suitable for, for example, conducting usability studies, collaborative usability studies, user experience testing, behavioral research, testing of commercial products and services, media testing, test compositing, and conducting test trials. Unlike previously known usability study labs, it allows parallel testing, reducing costs and increasing the relevance of comparisons between studies (**Figure 12**).

A laboratory for collaborative testing [3, 14, 16, 17, 20] characterized in that it comprises two substantially semicircular tables (1), each containing at least three workstations, each station containing a computer, a monitor (2) with a camera for capturing a user's face, a headset and a microphone, audio recording means, wherein the tables (1) are positioned such that the center of the imaginary circle of which the table (1) is a part faces the other table (1), and further, the axes of symmetry of the two tables (1) are parallel and offset from each other, and the monitors (2) of the workstations are arranged on each

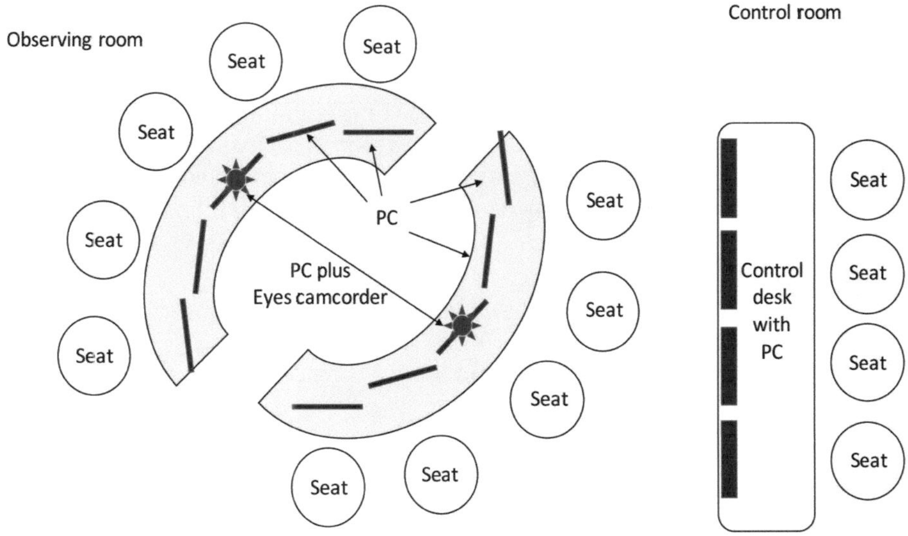

Figure 11.
Collaborative UI Lab [20].

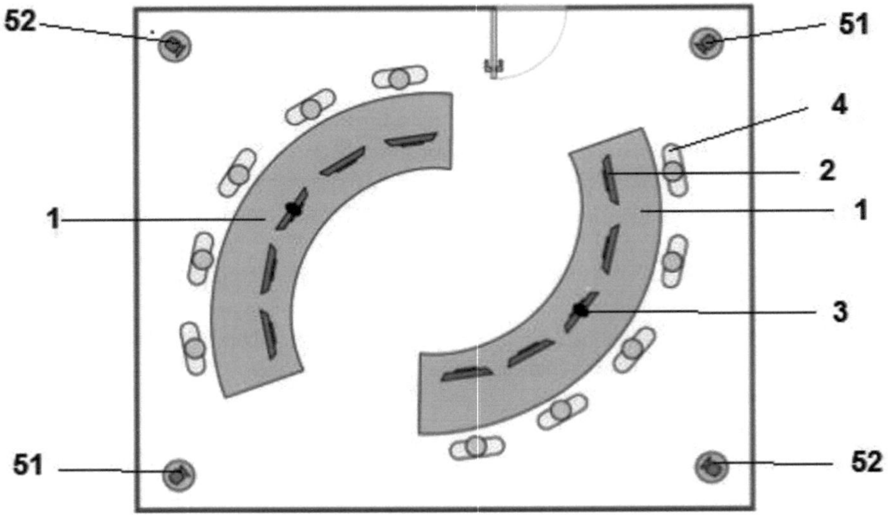

Figure 12.
Collaborative UI Lab description [20].

table (1) such that the screens are oriented away from the other table, wherein the central workstation of each table is provided with means (3) for tracking eye movements, and wherein the laboratory further comprises at least two speakers and at least four wide-angle cameras (51, 52), at least two of the cameras (52) being arranged to image the workstations including the screens of the monitors (2).

4.5 Remote testing

This is a very modern method of usability testing today. The UI Lab environment is replaced by the user's workstation. In fact, today's technology makes it possible to largely replace the classic UI Lab. Technology such as screen recording, voice recording, face capture, eye tracking (Gaze Recorder) is now commonly used. By connecting the workstation to the Internet, using today's On-Line technologies (Google Meets, MS Teams, Zoom, etc.), the workstation becomes part of a virtual lab. If the fact that the participant is not physically in the same room as the usability study facilitator can be managed or bridged, the test can be conducted. This approach has the following advantages as it is seen in **Table 8**.

4.5.1 Usability testing methods

Usability testing methods can be divided into two types: without users and with users.

Testing without users (called expert assessment):

- Heuristic evaluations [1, 2, 21]
- Cognitive walkthrough [1–3]
- Collaborative walkthrough [3, 14, 16, 17, 20]

Remote testing benefits
No need to build an expensive UI Lab.
The participant does not have to leave his/her place of work—saves time (which is an important factor). The participant does not have to leave his/her place of work—saves time (which is an important factor).
The participant conducts the test on his own equipment with which he is familiar (no orientation problems = advantages as in the In Situ approach).

Table 8.
Remote testing benefits.

4.6 Heuristic evaluation

Jacob Nielsen defined 10 general principles of machine-human interaction that a good user interface should support. These are general principles, which is why they are called "Heuristic." [1, 2, 21].

1. Visibility of system status
2. Match between system and the real world
3. User control and freedom
4. Consistency and standards
5. Error prevention
6. Recognition rather than recall
7. Flexibility and efficiency of use
8. Aesthetic and minimalist design
9. Help users recognize, diagnose, and recover from errors
10. Help and documentation

Allow us to quote them:

Visibility of system status:

- A system should not "freeze" and get unresponsive:
    - Show the progress bar.
- Inform the user what's going on, give a time estimate if >20 sec.

Match between system and the real world:

- Keep conventions and metaphors working:
    - Desktop.

- Icons must behave as expected:
    - Trash can—I can throw objects to a trash can, it can be emptied and also searched in case of accident.
- Beware of translation errors.

User control and freedom:

- Users often choose system functions by mistake:
    - Provide “emergency exit” from unwanted states.
- Undo.
- Allow canceling of time-consuming operations (rollback).
- Confirm actions which cannot be undone.
- Warn before action that cannot be undone.

Consistency and standards:

- Conventions of the platform should be obeyed.
    - Windows program looks and acts as a Windows program. No other way.
- Use just system components if possible.
- System colors and fonts.
- Use same terms and names:
    - Save vs. Write, etc.

Error prevention:

- The best error is the one which did not happen.
- User should not be able to enter an invalid value:
    - Following error message does not help that much.
- If the input requires some special form, it must be explained (in-line help text, hint):
    - Password strength/requirement.
- Highlight required fields in forms
- Confirm dialog where needed.

Recognition rather than recall:

- Only relevant objects and options are visible.
- The user is not requested to remember information.
- Give preview for visual selections (font).
- Step in a wizard (3 of 7).
- Position in a tree structure (bread crumb).

Flexibility and efficiency of use

- Provide keyboard shortcuts (accelerators).
- Accommodate both novice and power users:
    - Functionality required by power users is mostly not needed at all by standard users.
    - Advanced mode.
- Keyboard shortcuts/function keys.
- Macros, templates.
- Do we really need all that controls?

Aesthetic and minimalist design:

- Show only relevant information:
    - Each unit of information competes with all other units of information.
- Less options mean faster action.
- Avoid useless graphics.

Help users recognize, diagnose, and recover from errors:

- Best is not to get to the point where an error message is needed.
- Plain language error messagesno code, no abbreviations, etc.
- Precise indication and constructive suggestion of a solution.
- Should educate the user that the error is not repeated.

Help and documentation:

- System should be usable without any help
- The help is a must anyway
- Minimal, easy to search
- FAQs and examples are better than plain text
- Contextual help

Nielsen heuristics are designed for expert evaluation. This means that users are represented by experts. On the one hand, this results in fast and high-quality feedback on the usability of the UI. However, it is to keep in mind that this work cannot be done by a mere PC user.

4.7 Heuristic UI evaluation procedure – I/O

Focuses on the product as a whole—**Table 9**.

4.8 How to perform heuristic evaluation

Table 10 should be followed when performing the heuristic evaluation.
Heuristic Evaluation—report example—Table 11.
Heuristic evaluation form example
You need to find out, what precisely MDC (MyDreamCompany) can help with:

1. Go to Google and find the MDC company.
2. Visit the main page. What does the MDC's logo tell? (Analyze the Future)
3. What is the main message in the head banner? (Changing how the World Thinks).
4. Your boss gives you the task to contact the MDC managing director for your region—Asia:

    a. What is his/her name?

Inputs	Output
A user interface—working application, a prototype, even a screenshot	List of what violates these rules
Description of the target user group(s)	
Use-cases/scenarios	

Table 9.
Heuristic evaluation steps.

Step	Action
Tutorial	Explain the application to assessors (experts), provide a scenario if needed.

Evaluation	Individual experts perform the evaluation and record results (which law has been violated and how). For the testing is used **Testing scenario:**
	• Scenario is a realistic situation, where a person performs a list of tasks using the product being tested, while observers watch and take notes:
	  o Thinking aloud.
	• Use the most common or used scenarios.
	• Examples:
	  o Create an account in the system.
	  o Order a pair of jeans.
	Find information about a particular product.

Make Interview at the end (likes, dislikes, recommendation)	**"Perfect!", "I love it!"** is not a proper evaluation: • Some structure/framework needs to be defined. • Metrics need to be defined. • So that testers and designers of the UI can discuss the results. o Human behavior and actions are complex: • Difficult to analyze. • Individual difference. The interview is important to ask (careful order is important): • What you liked. • What you didn't like. • What are the recommendations.
Priority Assessment	Assess the severity of each problem.
Reporting	Discuss the conclusions with the assessors and design team.

Table 10.
Heuristic evaluation procedure.

Problem found	Error wiping
Violates:	4 Heuristic attribute -Consistency and Standards
Problem statement:	Strings "Save" and "Write File" refer to the same function. The users may be confused by this ambiguity.
Priority:	Medium (Usability problem, important to be removed).

Table 11.
Report example.

b. How many years of experience does (s)he have?

c. What was the his/her position prior to joining IDC?

5. What is his/her Twitter contact account?

Answers form [3] (**Figure 13**):

Heuristic evaluation form example. Not necessarily all 10 points are included. It depends on the focus of the test (**Figure 14**).

Answers ID	Fill the answer
2	
3	
4a	
4b	
4c	
5	

Figure 13.
Answer form for Heuristic evaluation example [3].

The options are weighted as follows

Yes	2
Partly	1
No	0

Heuristics	Score	Score in %	Values
Visibility of system status	4/4	100%	80 - 100%
Match between system and the real world	3/4	75%	60 - 80%
User control and freedom	4/4	100%	80 - 100%
Consistency and standards	0/4	0%	0 - 20 %
Error prevention	1/4	25%	20 - 40%
Recognition rather than recall	4/4	100%	80 - 100%
Flexibility and efficiency of use	2/4	50%	40 - 60%
Aesthetic and minimalist design	1/4	25%	20 - 40%
Help users recognize, diagnose, and recover from errors	3/4	75%	60 - 80%
Help and documentation	4/4	100%	80 - 100%

Figure 14.
Result of Heuristic Evaluation example [3].

4.9 Cognitive walkthrough

According to the Nielsen Norman Group, the Cognitive Walkthroughs is: [1, 2] "*a technique used to evaluate the learnability of a system from the perspective of a new user. Unlike user testing, it does not involve users (and, thus, it can be relatively cheap to implement). Like heuristic evaluations, expert reviews, and PURE evaluations, it relies on the expertise of a set of reviewers who, in a highly structured manner, walk through a task and assess the interface from a new user's point of view."*

Definition by Nielsen Norman Group [1, 2]: "*A cognitive walkthrough is a task-based usability-inspection method that involves a crossfunctional team of reviewers walking through each step of a task flow and answering a set of prescribed questions, with the goal of identifying those aspects of the interface that could be challenging to new users.*"

During the cognitive walkthrough, we ask ourselves the following questions:

- ***Will users try to achieve the right result?*** *In other words, do users understand that the action (step) at hand is needed to reach their larger goal?*

- ***Will users notice that the correct action is available?*** *In other words, is the interactive element that achieves the step visible or easily findable?*

- ***Will users associate the correct action with the result they're trying to achieve?*** *Perhaps the right button is visible, but will users understand the label and will they know to engage with it?*

- ***After the action is performed, will users see that progress is made toward the goal?*** *Based on what occurs after the action is taken, will users know that this action was correct and help them make progress toward their larger goal?*¨

Cognitive walkthrough is considered an appropriate method for testing user interfaces. Unlike heuristic evaluation, which looks in depth at general principles, cognitive walkthrough focuses more on the mental model of the user. That is, how the user interface interacts with his mental model. According to the authors' practice, the cognitive walkthrough more closely resembles reality. Therefore, the authors prefer it as a usability test (**Figure 15**).

Cognitive walkthrough - Zásilkovna example

	Will users understand how to start the task?	Are the controls understandable?	Will users know the control was the correct one?	Was there a feedback after completing the task?	Were you able to complete the task?	Notes
Create an account						
Open "Zásilkovna" app						
Click "Souhlasím a pokračovat"						
Enter your phone number						
Click "Pokračovat"						
Enter SMS code						
Fill in information about the package						
Click "Odeslat zásilku"						
Leave country of departure and target country as Czechia by clicking on "Pokračovat"						
Enter recipients' name in the "jméno" field						

Figure 15.
Cognitive walkthrough evaluation for Zasilkovna.cz example [3].

The method advantages	Criticism of the method
UI/UX bugs are found faster by a pair of participants than by an individual.	Opponents of the method blame the fact of cooperation. Collaboration can supposedly reduce the quality of answers. In other words, participants try less in pairs. Authors consider this statement to be a hypothesis that has not been confirmed.
If the UI behavior is non-standard, the pair will detect it faster. If the participant is not sure, he/she can ask a colleague. However, this advice (forbidden in classical studies) is a common help when evaluating SW in real-world settings. Therefore, the **First Time Experience** is better recognized.	
By collaborating on tasks, testing can be significantly accelerated.	
The overall interview is then carried out in a group where the synergy effect becomes apparent.	

Table 12.
The collaborative walkthrough method benefits.

4.10 Collaborative walkthrough

The collaborative passage is based on collaborative elements.

When author [20] constructed a collaborative usability lab at the Czech University of Life Sciences [19]) name HUBRU [20], also (J. Pavlicek) came up with the idea to implement a usability study based on the model of pair programming. The overall approach to this method is very similar to the cognitive walkthrough. The difference in principle is that a given task is performed by a pair of participants. This method, which authors (Pavlicek, Pavlickova et al. [14, 16, 17]) have been actively using since 2017, brings a number of benefits (**Table 12**).

4.11 Testing with users

It can be divided into:

4.11.1 User surveys

Potential users fill in or answer the questions in the questionnaire. The questionnaire has been prepared in advance and contains questions that are not instructional. Typically, the correct question is: "what is the appropriate background color for the XY application." An incorrect question is: "is green an appropriate background color for XY?" This question is incorrect because it mentally disqualifies green. An even more incorrect question would be a multiple choice question: is it better A) red, B) green, C) blue? Because one intuitively foregrounds the desired answer. Keep in mind the following fact: we DO NOT WANT to force our hypothesis by questioning, but to PROVE its existence. The survey should take no more than 45 min. The advantage of this method is that it can be done remotely. The number of participants should be more than 7 (as opposed to a qualitative usability study).

4.11.2 Ethnographic observations

Ethnographic observations—Table 13

Step	What to do
Observe users in their environment with no intervention and record and/or take notes.	Find out how people use the app etc.
Best if users do not know they are observed.	Ethically problematic
Contextual inquiry.	• Ethnographic approach. • Shorter: approx. 2–3 h. • Observing an experienced user of the app and taking notes. • To identify shortcuts, unexpected, interesting or confused reactions. • The participant knows about our presence.

Table 13.
Ethnographic observation.

4.11.3 Usability engineering

Usability engineering—Table 14

Step	What to do
Observing the users using the system in a simulated environment (usability lab).	
Wanted aspects of the real world are simulated.	
Users work on predefined, but realistic tasks.	
The environment should be as close to the real one as possible	Same system, same monitor(s), etc.

Table 14.
Usability engineering.

4.12 Collaborative usability engineering

Variant to usability engineering. It is again done in pairs or groups.

4.13 Variants of usability testing methods

In general, there are two basic methods of usability testing in terms of obtaining valid data. These are qualitative (generally the more common method suitable for Usability Labs) and quantitative. The latter is suitable for automated testing.

4.14 Qualitative

For the purpose of a qualitative usability study (usually testing with experts), five participants are sufficient (according to the Nielsen Norman Group) [1, 2, 21]. According to Nielsen, five participants will reveal 75% of UI bugs. Increasing the number of participants further does not yield a significant result. In authors'

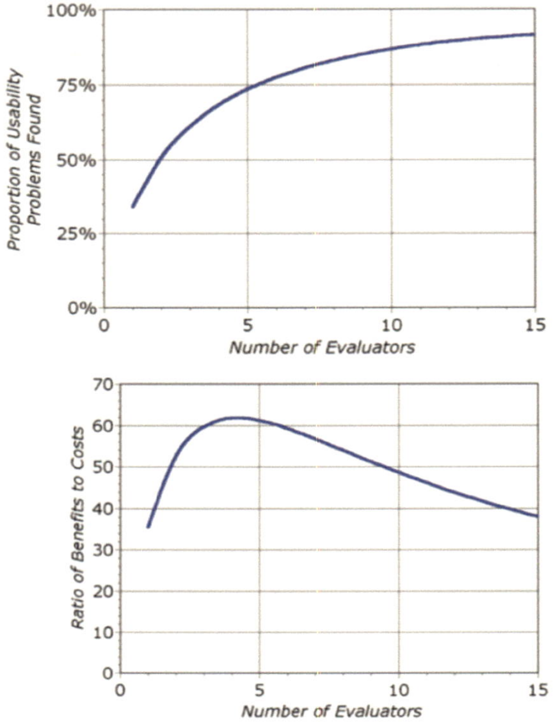

Figure 16.
How many participants is needed? [21].

experience, we prefer to recommend eight participants. The benefit of eight in ideal cases is not in the ideal ratio to five ones. But occasionally, it happens that a participant is delayed or disturbed by a phone call, and therefore, in our practice a number of 8 is safer. Respectively, it does not bring a fundamentally higher burden, and the result is safer (**Figure 16**).

4.15 Quantitative

A quantitative study is suitable for automated testing. They are generally generated from automated logs. That is, if the application collects and logs user behavior such as button clicks and user elements. This is quite common today with, for example, operating systems.

4.16 Define a story that explains the reason for testing

Tell the story of why the usability test is important. The story must be interesting and motivating for the participant to take the test.

4.17 Define a time frame

You should remember that the usability test should not take more than 30–45 min. Keep this in mind when planning scenarios. After 45 minutes, the participant will get tired. His/her ability to concentrate decreases, and the results are not relevant.

5. Summary (key results)

The principle of user interface design is a very artistic discipline. There are rules that partially prescribe how designers should proceed and what design patterns to follow. These are Look and Feel for different operating systems. And also, general rules for the placement of graphic elements, as the authors have already shown. On the other hand, there are market forces at work here. It is mandatory for a user interface designer to adhere to the prescribed Look and Feel. This is if he wants to place his solution in the Apple Store, for example. But at the same time, he needs to create a solution that is visually appealing and above all new. Copying the competition is not enough. Exclusivity is what sets it apart from the rest. Our users expect standard behavior from our solutions (the behavior they are used to). But at the same time, they want it to be innovative and attractive. It is called in the slang of interactional designers “sexy design.”

So let us summarize as follows:

- Collect user requirements for future solutions.
- Define the user tasks to be achieved.
- Divide them into atomic user goals (UseCases). Each task consists of a series of steps-user goals.
- Create personas or focus groups (these allow you to understand the mental model of the users).
- Based on the archetypal users (personas, etc.) and user tasks and goals, design UseCases. Always describe these from the user’s perspective.
- Start creating a specification in which you graphically represent the system screens-wireframes—in the form of sketches. These screens will be based on the user tasks. They will consist of individual (cumulative UseCases).
- Write scenarios for the wireframes. Write these from the system perspective so that they always satisfy the UseCases.
- Iterate the design process several times (e.g., three times).
- For wire models, create a Lo-Fi or Hi-Fi prototype.
- Create test scenarios from user goals.
- Based on the learned rules, conduct a usability study.
- Collect all flaws and fix the specification including the prototype.
- In the second usability test, all the shortcomings of the user interface design should already be eliminated.

Author notes

These figures 1,3,5,6,7 are drawn by Veronika Pavlickova daughter of Petra and Josef Pavlicek - authors of this article. These figures 2,8,9,11–15 are drawn by Petra and Josef Pavlicek authors of this article.

Author details

Josef Pavlíček* and Petra Pavlíčková
Department of Software Engineering, Faculty of Information Technology, Czech Technical University in Prague, Czech Republic

*Address all correspondence to: josef.pavlicek@fit.cvut.cz

References

[1] Nielsen J. Usability Engineering (Interactive Technologies). Morgan Kaufmann; 1993. ISBN-10: 0125184069

[2] Nielsen J. 1994. Available from: https://www.nngroup.com/ [Accessed: 31 May 2022]

[3] Pavlicek J. The Cookbook for Interaction Design and Human Computer Interaction. 2021. Available from: https://docs.google.com/presentation/d/1nbLjgEX5mS6kl_cRx6CeKuhd-fzz-kyYn_j03vMLkH4/edit?usp=sharing [Accessed: 31 May 2022]

[4] Jay W. Counterintuitive behavior of social systems. Theory and Decision. 1971;**2**:109-140

[5] Hick WE. "On the rate of gain of information" (PDF). Quarterly Journal of Experimental Psychology. 1952;**4**(1): 11-26

[6] Cockburn A, Gutwin C, Greenberg S. A predictive model of menu performance (PDF). In: Proceedings of the SIGCHI Conference on Human Factors in Computing Systems. San Jose, California; 2007. pp. 627-636

[7] Hyman R. Stimulus information as a determinant of reaction time. Journal of Experimental Psychology. 1953;**45**(3): 188-196

[8] Rosati L. How to design interfaces for choice: Hick-Hyman law and classification for information architecture. In: Slavic A, Salah A, Davies C, editors. Classification and Visualization: Interfaces to Knowledge: Proceedings of the International UDC Seminar. The Hague, The Netherlands; 2013. pp. 125-138

[9] Moggridge B. Designing Interactions. MIT University Press Group Ltd; 2006. ISBN13 (EAN): 9780262134743

[10] Crampton Smith G. Available from: https://www.linkedin.com/in/gillian-crampton-smith-27930b/?originalSubdomain=it [Accessed: 31 May 2022]

[11] Silver K. What Puts the Design in Interaction Design. 2007. Available from: https://www.uxmatters.com/mt/archives/2007/07/what-puts-the-design-in-interaction-design.php [Accessed: 31 May 2022]

[12] FOX. Available from: https://www.wired.com/2014/07/homer-simpson-car/) [Accessed: 31 May 2022]

[13] ISO Standard. Available from: https://en.wikipedia.org/wiki/Usability#ISO/TR_16982:2002_standard [Accessed: 31 May 2022]

[14] Pavlicek J, Rod M, Pavlickova P. Usability evaluation of business process modelling Standards–BPMN and BORM Case Study. In: In the International Conference on Advanced Information Systems Engineering. Cham: Springer; 2021. pp. 93-104

[15] Jacobson I. Use cases—Yesterday, today, and tomorrow. Software and Systems Modeling. 2004:210-220. DOI: 10.1007/s10270-004-0060-3

[16] Pavlicek J, Hronza R, Pavlickova P, Jelinkova K. The business process models quality metrics. In: Workshop on Enterprise and Organizational Modelling and Simulation. Cham: Springer; 2017. pp. 134-148

[17] Pavlicek J, Pavlickova P. Methods for evaluating the quality of process modelling tools. In: Workshop on Enterprise and Organizational Modelling and Simulation. Cham: Springer; 2018

[18] Available from: https://cent.felk.cvut.cz/courses/Y39TUR. [Accessed: 31 May 2022]

[19] Czech University of Life Sciences, Faculty of Management and Economics. Software Engineering Department. Available from: https://www.pef.czu.cz [Accessed: 31 May 2022]

[20] HUBRU. Available from: https://katedry.czu.cz/en/hubru/home [Accessed: 31 May 2022]

[21] Nielsen J. 1994. Available from: https://www.nngroup.com/articles/ten-usability-heuristics/ [Accessed: 31 May 2022]

Chapter 5

Usability Testing of Mixed Reality Scenarios: A Hands-on Report

Robert Strohmaier, Gerhard Sprung, Alexander Nischelwitzer and Sandra Schadenbauer

Abstract

We would like to share our insights in designing, preparing, preforming, and analyzing usability tests for multiple connected augmented reality and virtual reality applications as well as traditional mobile applications developed for a multimodal screening tool. This screening tool is under development at the University of Applied Sciences FH JOANNEUM in Graz, Austria. Several researchers from the departments of health studies and applied computer sciences are working closely together to establish a tool for early diagnosis of cognitive impairments to contribute to the management of dementia. The usability of this screening tool was evaluated by ten therapists paired with ten clients as testing group 1 and two usability experts in a separate test (group 2). In this chapter, we would like to describe why we use observed summative evaluation using the co-discovery method followed by post-task questionnaires for the first testing group. We are going to discuss the reasons for performing the cognitive walkthrough method as co-discovery with usability experts of testing group two as well. Furthermore, we describe how we use camera recordings (traditional cameras, 360-degree cameras), screen recording, and special tailor-made software to experience the screening process through the user's eyes.

Keywords: usability, user centered design, augmented reality, virtual reality, mixed reality, cognitive walkthrough, co-discovery, observation

1. Introduction

During this chapter we are going to discuss a usability study of a mixed reality scenario. Within the next pages, relevant literature is shown and insights into our ideas during planning of the usability study are given. As well as the subject of the test, the multimodal mixed reality scenario is going to be presented. In every section we tried to point out what is, in general, to do at a specific step or task during the usability processes. As well, we try to describe how we have done something (highlighted by the words "In our case") and, if applicable, we try to give suggestions, i.e., what can be improved (highlighted by the words "Potential for improvement").

First, we are going to clarify basic terms to establish a common understanding of the material at hand.

IntechOpen

When it comes to classifying an application into the areas of augmented reality (AR), virtual reality (VR), and mixed reality (MR), Vogel et al. gives a good overview of how these techniques are seen in different disciplines [1].

1.1 Augmented reality (AR)

In our remarks, we refer to the definitions of Azuma [2] and the virtuality continuum of Milgram [3]. AR has to fulfill the following three points:

- Virtual objects and virtual aid enrich the real environment
  The virtual objects and virtual aid have to be connected closely with the real environment. Virtual aid can be interpreted as visible content such as 3D models as well as invisible services like a digital tape measure to measure distances in the real environment.

- Anchored in real space
  In our point of view, it is important that virtual objects and services are anchored to the real environment. This connection has to be stable and must not change during the use of the application.

- Updates in real time
  All kinds of interactions should be computed in real-time. Furthermore, reactions to actions have to be rendered in real-time or, at least, with a minimal delay.

1.2 Virtual reality (VR)

Virtual reality can be seen as a completely virtual environment, where users are isolated from the real world and experience 3D models, spatial audio, and other digital content as well as other sensory stimuli. Ideally, the real world cannot be recognized at all. No real-world image, no real-world acoustic signal, no real-world smell, and no real-world tactile stimuli. Regarding the used hardware, this can be established completely or partly. Whereas using just a VR headset and moving within an environment like a therapist's treatment room, the immersion in the virtual environment is lesser. Regarding Milgram, we also tend to categorize our VR applications in the area of the virtual environment [4].

1.3 Mixed reality (MR)

Mixed reality is described as everything between the real and the virtual environment [3]. In addition, some major hardware and software companies tried to use this term to fit their hardware and software. In the following paragraphs, we are going to explain the elements of the conducted usability tests. All of them together are considered by us to be a mixed reality scenario.

1.4 Other important terms

Besides technical terms, during this chapter, we use many terms related to usability testing as well as terms related to the research project named SCOBES-AR (description of the project follows in the next section), itself. Therefore, within this section, we are going to clarify the meanings of the most important terms. In the case of any confusion about the used terms later on, please refer to this section.

- Usability test
  Structured process to assess how usable a computer-based system is.
- Usability method
  Determines how a usability test must be carried out. E.g., heuristic evaluation or thinking aloud can be seen as a usability method.
- Usability study
  If multiple usability tests are carried out to answer the same questions about the behavior of the users or the functionality of the product, we refer to this as a usability study.
- Expert (Usability expert)
  A person who possesses profound knowledge about usability.
- Facilitator
  A usability expert, who is in charge of planning, conducting, and analyzing usability tests.
- Observer
  A person with at least basic knowledge about usability assists the facilitator during usability tests. They are mainly in charge of observing the tests and taking notes.
- Participant
  A person who takes part in usability tests in the role of a user. This person must be recruited out of the target group(s) of the product to be tested. In our case, both therapists who are using the screening tool, as well as their clients being screened, can be participants in our usability study.
- Screening tool
  A set of different screenings to, in our case, test physical and cognitive abilities in healthy persons.
- Screening
  Activities to assess a person's abilities within a special scope (e.g. cognitive health, physical health).
- Task
  One step in screening.
- Therapist
  A health professional who offers some kind of health-related service. Therapist can utilize the screening tool developed by us.
- Client
  A client takes advantage of a health-related service, provided by a therapist. They can be screened by a therapist.

1.5 The Project SCOBES-AR

Cognitive impairments like dementia are a tremendous challenge for affected persons, their relatives, and for a country's health system. To detect cognitive impairments at a very early stage might bring a lot of advantages for people and for administration. Therefore, we are working on a multimodal screening tool (MST) to detect cognitive impairments early. After identifying suitable screenings, we try to advance these screenings by digitalizing them [5].

To accomplish these goals, we have developed multiple digital applications. Some of them fit into the area of AR, some of them into VR and others are simple digital applications running on smartphones and tablet computers. All AR, VR, and traditional digital apps form the digital screening tool. We see this combination as a mixed reality scenario. This is the reason for using the term MR in the title of this chapter. More information about the constituent applications, whether they are AR, VR, or just digital, is given in the next section.

2. Elements of the usability tests

This chapter's main focus lies on usability and usability test methods. Nevertheless, a short overview of the single applications which together make up the screening tool is given within this section.

Overall, the screening tool consists of several screenings. At the beginning of each screening, anamnestic data is collected with the help of questionnaires presented on websites. Those questionnaires are not subject to the usability test. We tried to focus on the AR, VR, smartphone and tablet applications, and the process they are used (see **Figure 1**).

During the whole process, therapists have to take care of clients, they have to start the right software at the right time, prepare the proper hardware and, in case of malfunctions, they have to troubleshoot. Because of that, handling the hardware is also subject of the usability tests.

With the application running on the tablet computer, therapists have to log into the client using a quick response (QR) code. Then, they can start and stop the screenings described below. They can also visually monitor everything the client sees in the AR and VR headsets. They are able to monitor and annotate the screenings (see **Figure 2**).

After this short description of the application used by the therapists, we are going to introduce the screenings, which are the subject of the usability tests (see **Figure 1**).

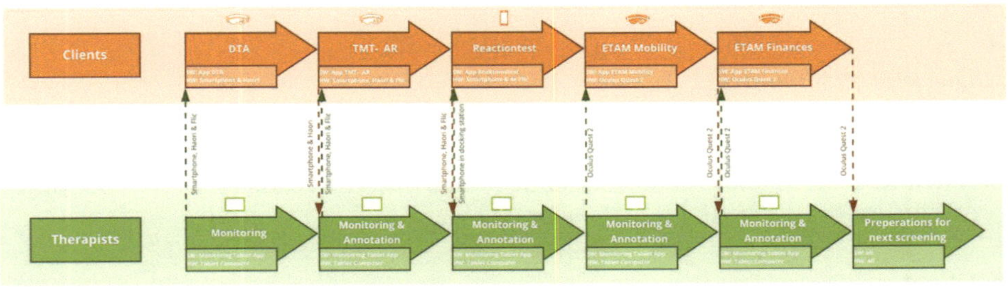

Figure 1.
Process of all screenings.

Figure 2.
Therapist during screening (monitoring and annotation).

2.1 Trail making test AR (TMT-AR)

Cognitive parameters are assessed during a process where clients have to select numbers and letters in ascending order [6, 7]. In the traditional form of the screening, these numbers are printed on a sheet of paper and pinpointed with a pencil, or the test is executed on a computer system.

In our case, numbers and letters are shown in virtual spheres, which are superimposed over the real world with the help of AR techniques. To accomplish this, the client wears a smartphone mounted in a Haori AR headset. To select single spheres, a flic2 button [8] is used. This can be seen in **Figure 3**.

2.2 Dual task assessment (DTA)

Gait parameters are measured by having the client walk a distance of 10 meters several times. If this screening were to be conducted traditionally, the distance would be marked on the floor. Therapists would use a stopwatch to measure elapsed time and would count the steps of the clients [9].

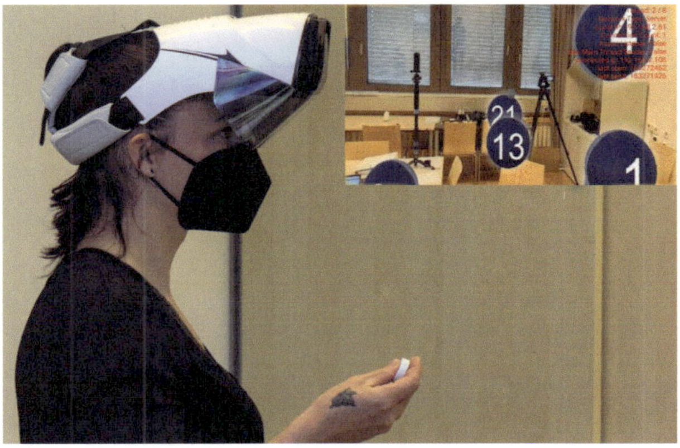

Figure 3.
Smartphone mounted in Haori headset worn by the client.

In our case, the client also wears a smartphone mounted in a Haori AR headset. A custom smartphone application utilizes AR techniques to measure distance, time, and footsteps.

2.3 Reaction test

During the traditional screening, reaction times of clients are measured by the talent diagnosis system (TDS) using the method "match 4 point" [10, 11].

In our case, a smartphone application is used to show visual stimuli. Depending on the stimulus, the client has to push the corresponding flic2 button. This application is just a smartphone app. No AR or VR techniques are used here.

2.4 ETAM mobility

The Erlangen test of activities of daily living in persons with mild dementia or mild cognitive impairment (ETAM) is carried out traditionally with printed pages. For the "mobility" element of this screening, clients are shown traffic scenes printed on paper. They have to argue about what people in these scenes are allowed to do [12].

In our case, clients wear an Oculus Quest 2 VR headset and find themselves within virtual environments, displayed as spherical 360-degree videos of traffic situations. Clients are able to look in all directions and have to interact with the system to decide where to go, when, and why (**Figure 4**).

2.5 ETAM finances

At this screening, the client's abilities regarding recognition of prices and mental arithmetic are measured. Traditionally the client has to decide which products to buy using a very simple fake catalog of a grocery store (**Figure 5**). In addition, money for a shopping list has to be calculated exactly with real currency units [12].

In our case, clients accomplished these tasks in a virtual shop wearing the Oculus Quest 2 VR headset.

After introducing the project SCOBES-AR and the single screenings of the screening tool, we'd now like to give an overview of some promising usability methods to test its user-friendliness.

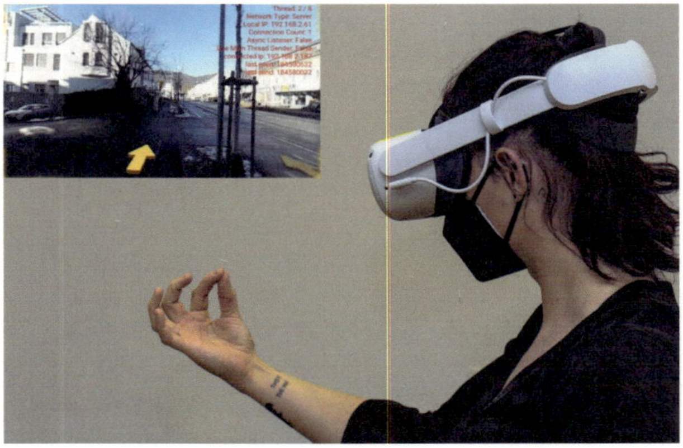

Figure 4.
ETAM mobility.

DOI: http://dx.doi.org/10.5772/intechopen.107792

Figure 5.
ETAM finances - view from inside VR headset.

3. Selection of suitable usability testing methods for AR and VR

Based on usability literature and our experiences we have preselected several usability testing methods. Those will be discussed, especially regarding their use in AR, MR, and VR settings, within this section. After reading the following paragraphs it will be clear which methods we have chosen and why.

At the beginning of every usability study, the selection of suitable usability testing methods takes place. Usability testing methods mostly originated during the rise of desktop software and websites. Nowadays the amount of AR and VR applications increases steadily. In tandem, attempts to test their usability become increasingly common. A good point to start from is recent papers and articles, in which usability studies of AR applications [13, 14] and of VR applications [15, 16] are presented or compared. Here, it is essential to know how traditional usability tests work. Authors like Barnum [17] and Nielsen [18] as well as practical guides [19] should be considered, before applying or adapting a usability method.

In our point of view, feedback from real users is essential to develop a meaningful product. Additionally, the detailed feedback of experts is needed, when real users cannot imagine what could be improved and how this could be achieved. In this case, well-experienced usability experts are very valuable. Hence, we designed two usability studies. The first is with methods suitable for real users and the second just to get feedback from usability experts.

During the next paragraphs, we would like to give a short overview of promising usability testing methods for this need. Along with this overview, we focus on the differences of the traditional method and the usage for AR, VR or MR.

3.1 Heuristic evaluation

According to Nielsen, heuristic evaluation is an expert tool, wherein usability professionals analyze a product regarding a set of 10 heuristics. Those heuristics cover a large amount of usability factors. Analyzing a product with this 10-point list determines if the product is giving proper feedback to the users, is oriented along real-world metaphors, provides helpful error dialogs, and many other aspects [18, 20, 21].

Those 10 heuristics are suitable for traditional desktop applications and websites. But, when it comes to other domains, some of them might not be suitable for the task at hand. For this reason, different researchers tried to adapt the heuristics for their own use. When it comes to VR, Sutcliffe and Gault came up with 12 heuristics [22] whereas Rusu et al. tried to introduce 16 heuristics [23] followed by a 9- point catalog of Murtza, Monroe, and Youmans [24]. When analyzing AR applications, Gale et al. suggest a 26 points catalog [25] and Endsley et al. compare different approaches [26].

Some of the recently developed heuristics are comparable with some of the 10 heuristics developed by Nielsen. Showing the system status to users, giving appropriate feedback, and helping to recover from errors are some points that are still important nowadays. Additionally, the newer heuristics are influenced mainly by factors of the AR and VR hardware like comfort of wearing the hardware and the immersion into a realistic (AR) or virtual (VR) environment.

Conducting a heuristic evaluation in the domains of AR, VR, and MR is challenging. A key factor in this challenge is considering the product to be tested and which heuristics to choose or how to alter some existing catalog of heuristics.

In our case, we have analyzed existing heuristics for AR and VR products. However, those heuristics were not suitable for us. As the process of developing a custom set of heuristics seemed to be out of the scope of the project, we rejected the idea of using heuristic evaluation.

3.2 Co-discovery

Evaluating products with two persons at the same time might be a very good idea. If two people are needed for the product or service, it is a good idea, to also test the usability with two people. This method can also be combined with other methods [17].

Furthermore, if the AR, MR, or VR product has to be operated by two people, co-discovery can also be used in such a scenario [14].

In our case, the method of co-discovery is a perfect match. Since as the scenario of our project consists of two people, the therapist and the client, who are working closely together, we decided to use co-discovery. We were also in favor of combining co-discovery with another method. These thoughts are described in the following paragraphs.

3.3 Thinking aloud

Following the thinking-aloud method, users must fulfill several tasks using a product. The product can be a physical object like a coffee machine or desktop software, or a website. The participants of the usability test are encouraged to think aloud and verbalize their mental models while interacting with the product [17, 18]. This enables deep insights into the usability of the product. Usability experts observe the completion of the tasks and the thoughts of the users. For documentation, the whole process is often filmed. By inviting 3 to 5 users, the main usability issues can be found. While this method can be seen as a cheap method it is very unnatural for participants to think out loud [18].

When it comes to AR, MR, and VR settings, this method also seems to be very promising. Interacting with virtual objects in real or virtual worlds while verbalizing thoughts seems to be a good solution. For example, Boulder et al. used the thinking-aloud method when comparing usability tests of a car infotainment system in an MR scenario and in a real scenario [27]. Thinking aloud might work in a broad range of AR, MR, and VR scenarios. On the other hand, the limitations of the method have to be considered. For example, if speech recognition is used to interact with the product, thinking aloud is inappropriate and may lead to accidental input. It must also be considered that thinking aloud produces a cognitive load on the side of the participants which can influence the results of a usability study.

In our case, it is crucial to get direct feedback from real users. Thinking aloud appeared to be a promising approach to accomplish this. But, as far as clients must carry out physical and especially cognitive screenings, we have seen huge problems in the thinking-aloud method. As well, usability tasks in addition to the tasks of the screening would be overwhelming for the clients and the therapists. Because of these reasons we did not apply this method to our usability studies.

3.4 Observation

The aim of observations is to study the users working with a product in a natural environment while not interrupting or disturbing them. Besides taking notes to gather qualitative feedback, videos can be recorded to analyze the observations. In some cases, the users can be interrupted to answer questions. According to Nielsen, three or more users have to be observed to get meaningful results [17, 18].

Because of the simple and product-independent setup, observations can also be conducted when evaluating AR [14, 28], MR, and VR products. Gaining qualitative feedback and impressions of the usage under normal conditions seems to be very promising.

In our case, observation fulfilled our requirements. It combines the view of real users doing everything which is needed for the real screenings without any influences of usability methods. Therefore, we applied this usability test method together with the co-discovery method. Therapist and client can perform a screening under realistic conditions while being observed to gather meaningful results regarding the usage of the different software applications and the process itself.

3.5 Questionnaires

Questionnaires can help to get structured feedback from participants before, during, and after a usability test. How many questionnaires to use and what they look like, is mostly defined by the product to be tested and the current stage of the product lifecycle. Questionnaires can be answered by the participants before (pretest), during (posttask) and after (posttest) a usability test. Whereas pretest questionnaires often aim to get more background information about potential users, posttask questionnaires relate directly to the completion of single tasks. Finally, posttest questionnaires are closely related to the goals of the full usability test [17, 19, 29].

When it comes to analyzing VR applications, VRUSE is an early attempt to provide a set of 100 questions structured in 10 parts [30]. Rather than answering the VRUSE questions within a Microsoft Excel spreadsheet, Putze et al. suggests implementing the questionnaires directly into the VR application. Here the questions are displayed within the virtual world, and they can be answered by using the VR controller, which is also used for the main application [16].

When using this approach in VR or AR persons with sight impairment must be considered. Besides, the implementation of a questionnaire into AR or VR software needs more resources as handling it like a traditional questionnaire.

Questionnaires can also be applied for AR applications. A good point to start research in this area is the overview provided by Pranoto et al. [14].

In our case, we have decided to use questionnaires after each usability observation to figure out if the perception of the usability test facilitator matches the self-perception of the participants. Considering the target groups and the duration of the whole screening process, we tried to come up with a simple and rather short questionnaire. We've analyzed the VRUSE questionnaire [30] and selected the following important aspects for the project SCOBES-AR:

1. Functionality
2. User input
3. Help and user manual
4. System output
5. Hardware
6. Immersion

According to these considerations we composed a set of questions. For each screening, the questions looked similar. This enabled us to draw conclusions between screenings. Because of the small sample of 10 therapists and 10 clients as participants, documentation was done in Microsoft Excel. This sample size is too small to draw conclusions from the questionnaires itself. However, in combination with the documentation of the observations, the questionnaires are able to help us to better understand what participants did and why they did it.

3.6 Cognitive walkthrough

When it comes to analyzing whether users are able to interact with a system in a proper manner, a cognitive walkthrough can be conducted. Inspecting especially the learnability of a system, action sequences are analyzed by usability experts. To be successful, the experts need information about the users of the system, and typical tasks for the system must be prepared. During the usability test, four main questions are being considered:

- Will the user try to get the right result?
- Will the user notice that the right action is available to them?
- Will the user associate the correct action with the expected result?
- When the right action is taken, will the user see progress being made toward the intended outcome?

Based on this analysis, suggestions were made on how to improve usability [17, 21, 31].

The main key is, whether using it for traditional digital products or AR or VR products, to make sure that the experts understand the users. This might be solved by personas and empathy maps, which can be created on the basis of focus groups [17–19, 31].

This method can just as well be used in AR, MR, and VR scenarios. The method may be altered slightly, but also can be utilized as described for other digital products [14, 15].

In our case, the expert view regarding those questions was exactly what we needed. To take into account the fact that at a real screening therapist and client work in pairs, we applied the cognitive walkthrough in form of a co-discovery.

After this discussion of usability methods, we are going into detail. Within the next section, the most important steps in preparing the usability studies are detailed. Please be aware, that more details can be found in usability literature.

4. Preparation phase

During this chapter, we explain the most important steps in designing a usability study. We will cover mainly the steps we have used for our study design and mention some other methods in short. Additionally, we will describe our lessons learned while designing the study for the mixed reality scenario.

4.1 Important documents

Usability experts suggest writing a guideline document for every usability test. Every consideration should be documented within this guideline. As well, all considerations during planning phase can be documented here.

Most times also a general data protection regulation (GDPR) [32] consent is needed where participants agree to the computation of their private data. Depending on the type of study and individual regulations in different countries, other documents like a data management plan and others might also be needed. Country depended regulations [33] must be met [17].

In our case: We've written an independent guideline for each usability study. Apart from goals, ideas, and to-do lists, the exact timetables of the usability tests were especially useful. Very helpful as well as contacting a law expert when it comes to documents relating GDPR. This step is strongly recommended.

4.2 What is the aim of the usability study?

The most important step in preparing the tests is to identify the aim(s) of the usability tests. Depending on the aim(s), different usability testing methods are suitable and different kinds of participants must be recruited. Also, the methods of documentation and presentation vary [17].

In our case: We wanted to see how clients and therapists handle the software and how they interact with each other. The typical usability of the software and the overall screening process had to be evaluated.

4.3 Recruitment of participants

Next should be considered whether the real users out of the target group(s) should be involved in the usability test, or if usability experts should analyze the product(s). Enough time for recruiting participants should be planned. Regarding the sample size, this step can take a long time. The number of participants strongly varies depending on the usability test method. For detailed information please have a look at the literature within chapter 3: Selection of Suitable Usability Testing Methods [17].

In our case: We wanted both the expert view and insights from the target groups. Therefore, we conducted two usability studies. The first study was conducted with 10 therapists and 10 clients, who worked together in pairs. The second study took place with two usability experts, one of them took over the role of the therapist and the other the role of the client.

It is good practice to inform participants during recruitment on the phone about what will happen during the usability tests (e.g., if they will be recorded with video cameras and microphones) and especially about GDPR. If this is not done in the worst case a participant shows up and does not agree to be recorded. In this case, the test ends before it begins, and the time of every person involved is wasted. Some of our participants stated at the beginning of the tests that they feel a little bit uncomfortable when being filmed. However, every participant agreed to sign the GDPR document. If they would not be informed beforehand, during the recruitment phase, some of them maybe would refuse to cooperate right at the beginning of the test.

4.4 Selection of the usability test personnel

The consideration about who should lead and observe the usability tests should be taken right at the beginning of the planning phase. Deep knowledge of usability testing is strongly needed especially for the facilitator. Ideally, the whole of the usability personnel contributes during the planning phase. As well it should be decided who is responsible for analyzing the findings after the usability tests [17].

In our case: We have decided to run the tests with just one person. Aside from other reasons, limited resources led us to this decision. This means the facilitator was in charge of all interactions with the participants, doing observations during the usability tests, and handling the hardware. Doing so can be described as possibly stressful for the facilitator. However, it is feasible. Simply ensure that this person is very well prepared and can handle hardware and malfunctions of the hardware in proper time by themself.

Potential for improvement: If two or more participants work together on a usability test at the same time, each one should be observed by one distinct observer. The facilitator might take on the role of one observer in such a scenario. Activities like preparing documents or preparing the hardware and product(s) used in the usability test can be shared between those persons. In any case, observing the participants should be shared. Focusing on one participant while taking notes has a huge potential in increasing the quality of the notes whilst also reducing the time spent during analysis of the notes after.

4.5 Defining the usability test methods

The aim(s) of the usability study and the product to be tested has a huge impact on choosing the right testing method. Also, choosing more than one testing method can lead to improved results. Because of the variety of available testing methods and the novelty of testing methods for AR and VR this selection process is described in detail in chapter 3: Selection of Suitable Usability Testing Methods.

4.6 Defining the tasks

After deciding these details, the tasks of the usability studies and/or the questions of the questionnaires must be defined. Depending on the selected testing method(s) and the product to test, the tasks that the participants of the usability study have to accomplish are very different. Always keep the aim(s) of the study in mind when it comes to creating the tasks.

Besides defining the tasks, it can also be necessary to prepare additional information. When using an expert usability method, it might be essential to present results of personas, empathy maps, or similar tests to them.

In our case: In usability study one, we wanted the therapists and clients to act as they do normally during such a screening. Therefore, no specific tasks were defined. The only task was to do the screening. Therapists were introduced to the screening tool in advance and most of them had also done several screenings before the usability test. The clients are instructed by the therapists and do not have to have special knowledge about the screening methods.

When it comes to the expert test, the whole story looks a little bit different. The usability experts do not have knowledge about the screening methods. Nor do they have domain knowledge in the field of the therapists like physical therapy, occupational therapy, dietetics, or speech therapy. To make them familiar with the screenings, the screening method itself and the therapeutic background were explained. Special functions regarding the software were not. As well they have to be provided with detailed information about the target groups in the form of personas and empathy maps.

Besides thinking about tasks themselves, how the task completion can be measured and evaluated has to be considered as well during the preparation phase. In our case, we gathered qualitative data during the observation and categorized it with a coding scheme, and prioritized them by importance and urgency (see 6.3 Notes of the Observations and Codes).

When questionnaires will be used, the questions should be developed during the planning phase. A scale to rate the answers must also be defined. As a scale we used a five-level Likert scale with the following items:

Strongly disagree - Disagree - Neither agree nor disagree - Agree - Strongly agree.

4.7 Defining the documentation method(s)

Last but not least, during preparation, the documentation and analysis of the usability studies have to be considered. It's important to get an overview of needed hardware and software. As well it is an important step in planning to decide, when and where to place which camera(s). This is going to be discussed in Section 6 Documentation and Analysis.

After writing about the preparation phase, we describe in the next section, how we have carried out the usability tests.

5. Carrying out the usability tests

Below we try to give an overview of steps, which were very important for our usability studies. Again, like in the previous sections, more detailed information can be found in usability literature written by Barnum [17] or Nielsen [18]. The focus of this chapter stays on a hands-on report, where we try to show what we have done and why.

5.1 Usability study 1: observed summative evaluation

The first usability study was done in the form of an observation followed by a posttest questionnaire. It was combined with screenings under real conditions.

10 therapists and 10 clients were recruited for the usability tests. They had been informed about GDPR in advance and were willing to be filmed when they arrived. Starting with an introduction to usability and the reasons for the usability study, the facilitator activated all the video cameras and screen recorders. By clapping his hands, the audio signal for synchronization was given. Retreated to the background, the facilitator started taking notes. From screening to screening the facilitator had to change the positions of the cameras. The rest of the time, he tried to be in the background not influencing the screening.

After the screenings, a posttest questionnaire was handed out, where therapists and clients got different questions. The aim of the questionnaires was to gather additional feedback and to better understand the actions taken by the users during the usability test.

Potential for improvement: It might be better if every person who is to be observed would get a distinct observer. Observing two persons at a time is possible. But more detailed notes can be taken, if one observer can concentrate on a single user.

5.2 Usability study 2: cognitive walkthrough as a Co-discovery

As mentioned before, cognitive walkthrough was chosen as a method to gain deep insights into the usability from experts. Because of the fact that during the screenings therapists work in pairs with their clients, the method of co-discovery was also utilized. So, two usability experts were invited to analyze the product using the method of a cognitive walkthrough working in pairs, which is typical for the co-discovery method.

The agenda of the cognitive walkthrough was quite tough. All of the four screenings which utilize AR and VR have to be tested by experts. The experts themselves have profound knowledge about usability, computer science, interaction design, and didactics. But what they do not have is knowledge about medicine, health care, and traditional screening methods. Therefore, they must be introduced to every single screening, while not showing them too much detail about the software before the usability test starts. In doing this, the facilitator followed this outline, whereas 0x is a placeholder for all 4 screenings. So those three parts are carried out 4 times in the test.

- Introduction to the project
- Introduction to the personas and empathy maps
- Introduction to screening 0x
- Carrying out screening 0x
- Discussion about the main issues during screening 0x
- Closing remarks

While the screening took place, everything was filmed by a screen recorder with an activated microphone in the therapist's tablet computer. Notes were taken by the facilitator during the screenings as well as during the discussion of each screening. During the phase of discussing a screening, the screen recording was very valuable. Uncertainties during the discussion about what was happening before the screening could be clarified easily.

A very important point to discuss when planning the agenda are the breaks. The whole usability test session took us about 6 hours. It is really hard for the experts and for the facilitator to stay focused. A coffee break, some sweets and a lunch with time for networking were very important to stay on task.

More detailed information about the process of the cognitive walkthrough itself can be found in the next section, where one of the usability experts outline his experiences during the test.

Potential for improvement: At the beginning, special terms which are used within the product should be presented and clarified. A small, printed dictionary might help a lot, too, when wording is not clear.

It turned out, that during expert tests the experts also tend to give feedback about the usability test itself. One of their suggestions was given in relation to the empathy maps. Those should be extended to mood boards, where personas can be seen in different situations which are important for the product. Grouping and categorizing feelings take a very important place as well and should be designed in a proper way.

The section below is written by one of the participating usability experts and should give insights into the perspective of the experts during the usability test.

5.3 Impressions from participating usability experts

The task was to review the usability of the dashboard application used by therapists and the applications used by the clients during a screening. Furthermore, the communication and interaction between therapists and clients have to be assessed.

Right at the beginning of the usability test, it became clear that a lot of used terms were not clear at all. Wording is a very important point in communication.

We have to take into account a large number of different roles and needs, wishes, and fears associated with them. The roles that we two usability experts are supposed to assume are extremely differentiated. The introduction to the personas was essential to conducting the cognitive walkthrough. The phase of discussing persona descriptions and empathy maps took much longer than planned. The facilitator accepted these circumstances and altered the complete test schedule on the fly. Without deep knowledge about the target groups, the whole test might be completely senseless. Accordingly, it is a very unusual constellation in which a conventional setup would not have the desired success.

After studying and discussing personas and empathy maps in detail, we decided to change roles after each screening. This decision was made because our experiences in AR and VR methods were seen as helpful for the test settings. Also, more precise and differentiated findings were expected. This alternation was very helpful to act and discuss on a meta-level. Therefore, discussions not only about one single screening were held. Moreover, the complete screening tool was present during all steps of the usability test and was evaluated and accessed as a whole product.

6. Documentation and analysis

When it comes to taking notes using a coding scheme, recording several videos of the observation, synchronizing all the media created during the usability tests, and documenting and presenting the gathered and aggregated data, special usability testing software can be very handy. Unfortunately, when using usability software, costs emerge most times. If the budget for usability tests is severely limited, and you are familiar with spreadsheet software like Microsoft Excel or something similar, you can use that software to design customized observation sheets, which is shown later. In the following section, the process of taking videos for documentation and analysis purposes will be discussed.

6.1 Interactions in the real world

Depending on the format of documentation, different pieces of hardware, like video cameras, microphones, and software (like special screen recorders) are needed. If interactions in a real environment are important, digital video cameras can be used. If interactions are distributed around in the real environment, a camera that can record spherical 360-degree video [34–36] of a whole scene at once might prove to be very useful [18].

In our case, we were interested in task completion in the smartphone, tablet, AR, and VR applications. It was very important for us to see the connection between tasks in the software and interaction in the real environment. Therefore, interactions in the real environment were recorded by two cameras facing each other to cover the whole test area. Additionally, we recorded spherical 360-degree video with the Ricoh Theta Z1 [37]. For each screening, the setting, shown as an example in **Figure 6**, has to be adapted a little bit.

But, recording video in the real world is not enough, when it comes to testing the usability of AR and VR scenarios.

6.2 Seeing through the users eyes

To see what users see is essential to understand interactions of users acting in AR and VR Applications. In the area of VR applications, screen recording software is sufficient most of the time. Hardware like the Oculus Quest 2 allows screen recording directly in the menu of the headset [38].

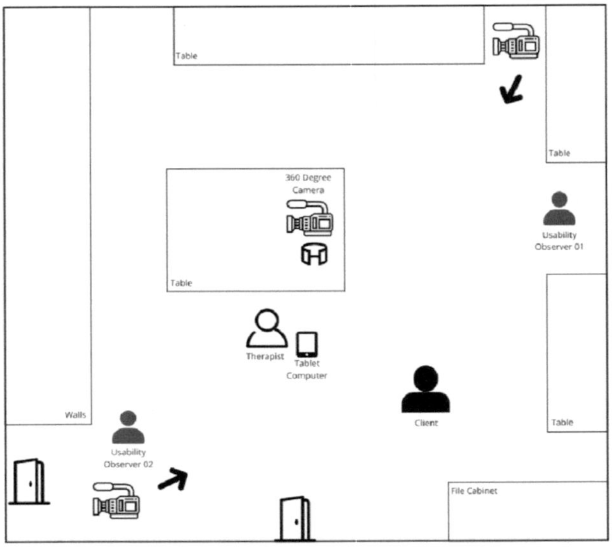

Figure 6.
Positions of the video hardware for the VR screenings.

DOI: http://dx.doi.org/10.5772/intechopen.107792

When thinking about AR scenarios, screen recorders reach their limits. Depending on the techniques used to superimpose the real world, screen recorders might not be able to be used. When working with optical see-through devices like the Microsoft Hololens a technique called spectator view comes into account. This technique allows us to record not only the virtual objects rendered into the sight of users but rather the whole virtual and real environment [39].

In our case, when it comes to interaction with the software, we have used Android's built-in screen recording tool on the therapist tablet computer. This solved two problems at once: within this screen recording we can reconstruct when which button was pressed by the therapist. As well, due to the fact that the therapist sees inside the tablet software exactly what the client sees, the view through the user's eyes is also recorded without any further screen recording software.

After the usability tests, the video material of all cameras must be synchronized and put together in a single video (**Figure 7**). A situation where this is not possible is with spherical 360-degree videos. They need special players to be shown most times. Synchronization of traditional recorded videos and screen videos works well with simple audio signals like clapping hands several times. Therefore, the microphones for each video camera and the ones connected to screen recorders must be activated. The step of synchronization should be done, to have one single video stream to have a look at, when the notes, which are going to be described in the next section, show interesting behavior.

6.3 Notes and codes

Before taking notes, a coding scheme should be created. As a coding scheme, we usually see a short description (1 or 2 words) or title to help to categorize all possible different findings during the usability observation. It can be very helpful to discuss

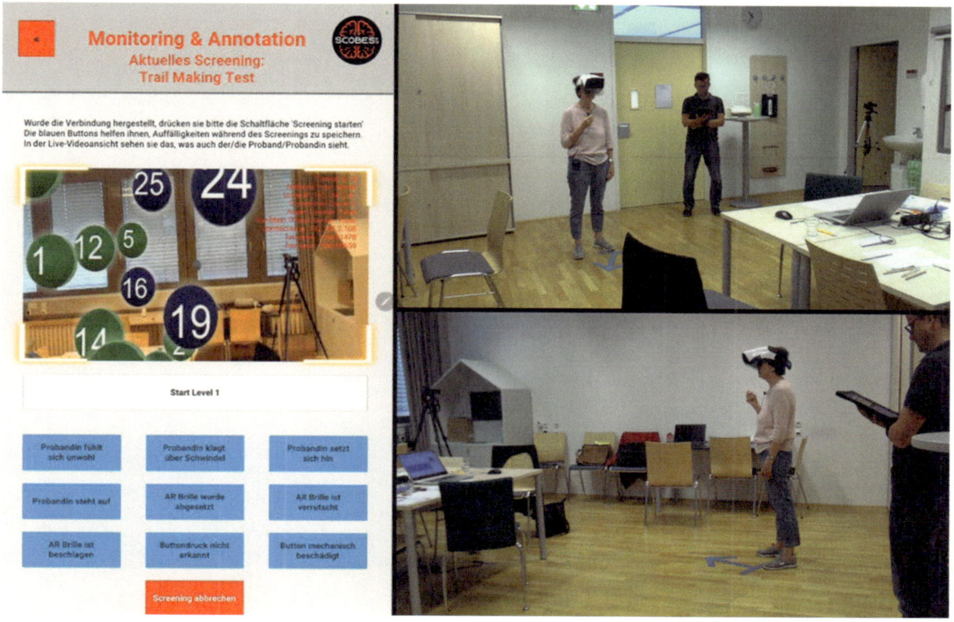

Figure 7.
All video-streams combined.

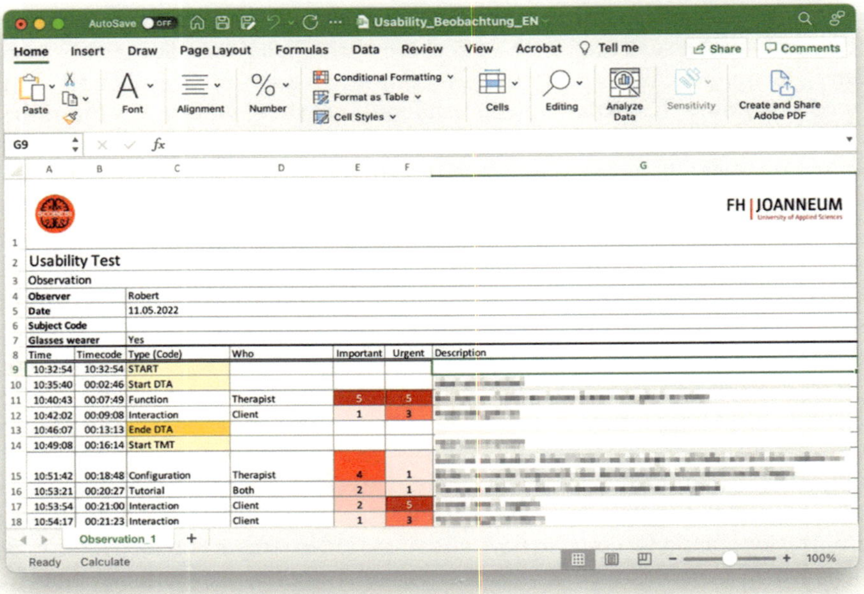

Figure 8.
Suggested use of excel spreadsheet for observations.

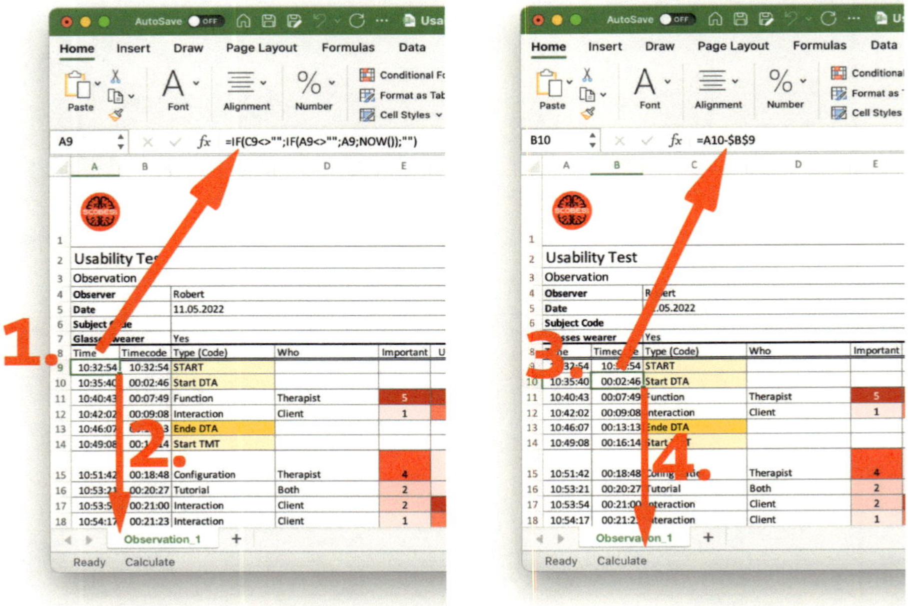

Figure 9.
Automatic creation of timestamps.

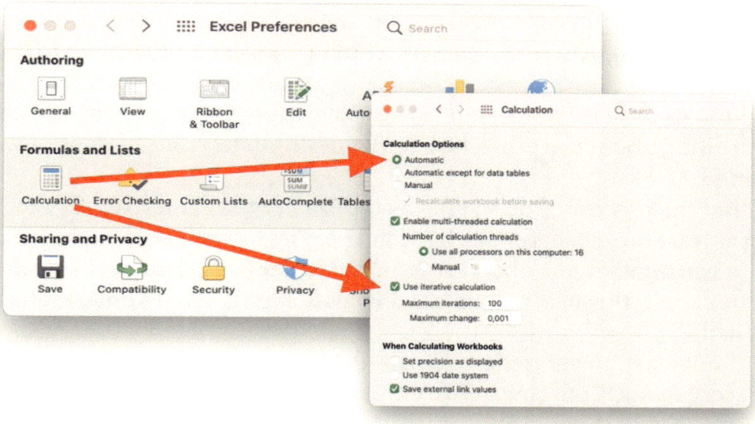

Figure 10.
Calculation options.

these codes with the development and usability team. Here, a pre-test is essential, to test and alter the coding scheme if necessary. Most times it is necessary.

The structure illustrated in **Figure 8** was very helpful for us. In column A the time of day was entered automatically when the code of the observed item was entered in the cell in column C. As well, based on the start time of the observation (cell A9) the corresponding timecode was calculated and entered automatically in the corresponding cell in column B. How to accomplish these two calculations in Microsoft Excel (Version 16.62 for Macintosh computers) is shown in **Figure 9**. The Timecode is extremely important when it comes to analyzing the video recordings. As mentioned in the section about the documentation using video an acoustic signal can be used to synchronize the recordings. At the moment of this signal, the first code (code START) has to be entered in column C9. From now on, the timecode of the observations is exactly the same as the timecode of the documentation of the video recordings.

If the calculations are not executed immediately after entering the code in column C, open Excel preferences and set in the menu calculation the calculation option to automatic. The option "Use iterative calculation" should be activated too. Otherwise, a warning about circular references might prohibit entering values. The appropriate setting for both options is illustrated in **Figure 10**.

7. Conclusions

Analyzing usability is a challenging task, whether the item to test is a traditional desktop application or a hardware-intensive MR scenario. Traditional usability methods, like the ones presented in this chapter, are useful and established. So, also for new purposes like AR, VR, and MR the traditional methodologies can be very helpful, at least as a starting point for research on new methods or to alter traditional methods to fit the items to test.

Furthermore, seeing through the user's eyes has a tremendous impact on usability studies, when it comes to testing usability of AR, VR, and MR applications and scenarios. We were sure that it is crucial for the whole project, that therapists can exactly see what clients see. But, also for the analysis of the usability studies, it was extremely helpful to watch the screen recording of the tablet software, where the viewport of the clients was shown. It assisted us in discussing usability issues with the experts after each screening.

In addition to that, we must emphasize, how important it is to inform participants during recruiting about the procedure of the usability test and, if applicable, that they will be filmed.

Regarding the process of observing a co-discovery, we can strongly recommend recruiting at least one observer per participant. The facilitator can take both roles, of course, ensuring that one observer is available per participant. The needs of the participants can, in this manner, be handled easier and observation results may be more detailed.

Last but not least, never underestimate the importance of detailed and lively persona descriptions. Combined with empathy maps they are a great tool, to help someone to take over the role of users from the target group(s). And, as the usability experts stated, empathy maps and personas can be enriched by pictures in the style of a mood board.

Acknowledgements

We'd like to thank all of our colleagues at the University of Applied Sciences FH JOANNEUM, who worked enthusiastically on the project SCOBES-AR and enabled the creation of the screening tool as well as the development of the software and the usability studies. Beginning with the project manager Wolfgang Staubmann, all other colleagues are presented in alphabetical order: Hannes Aftenberger, Konrad Baumann, Monica Christova, Theresa Draxler, Brigitte Loder-Fink, Bernhard Guggenberger, Ulrike Hauser, Nina Maas, Bianca Fuchs-Neuhold, Christoph Palli, Rene Pilz, Lucia Ransmayr, Helmut Simi, Anna Steiner, and Elisabeth Url.

As well we'd like to thank our students Miriam Grainer, Stefan Krasser, Lukas Bichler, Gerhard Zwitkovits and Andreas Krejan, who developed very helpful prototypes as starting points for the screening tool.

For proofreading and important remarks, we'd kindly like to thank Skye Sprung.

Finally, we thank the Austrian Institute of Technology for providing the backend system and securely hosting the collected data.

The project SCOBES-AR is funded by the Austrian Research Promotion Agency (FFG) under grant number 866873.

Author details

Robert Strohmaier*, Gerhard Sprung, Alexander Nischelwitzer
and Sandra Schadenbauer
FH JOANNEUM, Institute of Business Informatics and Data Science, Graz, Austria

*Address all correspondence to: robert.strohmaier@fh-joanneum.at

References

[1] Vogel J, Koßmann C, Schuir J, Kleine N, Sievering J. Virtual- und augmented-reality-definitionen im interdisziplinären Vergleich. In: Thomas O, Ickerott I, editors. Smart Glasses. Berlin, Heidelberg: Springer Berlin Heidelberg; 2020. pp. 19-50

[2] Azuma R. A survey of augmented reality. Presence: Teleoperators and Virtual Environments. 1997;**6**(4):355-385

[3] Milgram P, Takemura H, Utsumi A, Kishino F. Augmented reality: A class of displays on the reality-virtuality continuum. In: 1995 SPIE Proceedings Vol. 2351: Telemanipulator and Telepresence Technologies. Boston, MA. 1995. pp. 282-292

[4] Jerald J. The VR Book: Human-Centered Design for Virtual Reality. New York, San Rafael, California: Association for Computing Machinery Morgan & Claypool Publishers; 2016

[5] FH Joanneum Gesellschaft mbH. Mixed Reality Prototype of Multimodal Screening for Early Detection of Cognitive Impairments in Elderly: Protocol Development and Usability Study [Internet]. clinicaltrials.gov; 2022. Report No.: NCT05403814. Available from: https://clinicaltrials.gov/ct2/show/NCT05403814

[6] Tischler L, Petermann F. Trail making test (TMT). Zeitschrift für Psychiatrie, Psychologie und Psychotherapie. 2010;**58**(1):79-81

[7] Rasmusson DX, Zonderman AB, Kawas C, Resnick SM. Effects of age and dementia on the trail making test. The Clinical Neuropsychologist. 1998;**12**(2): 169-178

[8] Flic 2|The Smart Button for Lights, Music, Smart Home and More. Flic Smart Button. 2022. Available from: https://flic.io/

[9] Hunter SW, Divine A, Frengopoulos C, Montero OM. A framework for secondary cognitive and motor tasks in dual-task gait testing in people with mild cognitive impairment. BMC Geriatrics. 2018;**18**(1):202

[10] TDS Hardware 2011. 2022. Available from: http://www.werthner.at/tds/tds-german/tds-hardware1.htm

[11] TDS Test Stand 2011-11. 2022. Available from: http://www.werthner.at/tds/tds-german/tds-test1.htm

[12] Luttenberger K, Reppermund S, Schmiedeberg-Sohn A, Book S, Graessel E. Validation of the Erlangen test of activities of daily living in persons with mild dementia or mild cognitive impairment (ETAM). BMC Geriatrics. 2016;**16**(1):111

[13] Merino L, Schwarzl M, Kraus M, Sedlmair M, Schmalstieg D, Weiskopf D. Evaluating Mixed and Augmented Reality: A Systematic Literature Review (2009-2019). In: 2020 IEEE International Symposium on Mixed and Augmented Reality (ISMAR). Porto de Galinhas, Brazil: IEEE; 2020. pp. 438-451

[14] Pranoto H, Tho C, Warnars HLHS, Abdurachman E, Gaol FL, Soewito B. Usability Testing Method in Augmented Reality Application. In: 2017 International Conference on Information Management and Technology (ICIMTech). Yogyakarta: IEEE; 2017. pp. 181-186

[15] Karre SA, Mathur N, Reddy YR. Usability Evaluation of VR Products in Industry: A Systematic Literature Review.

In: Proceedings of the 34th ACM/SIGAPP Symposium on Applied Computing. Limassol Cyprus: ACM; 2019. pp. 1845-1851

[16] Putze S, Alexandrovsky D, Putze F, Höffner S, Smeddinck JD, Malaka R. Breaking the Experience: Effects of Questionnaires in VR User Studies. In: Proceedings of the 2020 CHI Conference on Human Factors in Computing Systems. Honolulu, HI, USA: ACM; 2020. pp. 1-15

[17] Barnum CM, editor. Usability Testing Essentials. 2nd ed. Morgan Kaufmann; 2021

[18] Nielsen J. Usability Engineering. San Diego, CA: Academic Press; 1993

[19] Richter M, Flückiger MD. Usability und UX kompakt. Berlin, Heidelberg: Springer Berlin Heidelberg; 2016

[20] Experience WL in RBU. 10 Usability Heuristics for User Interface Design. Nielsen Norman Group. 2022. Available from: https://www.nngroup.com/articles/ten-usability-heuristics/

[21] Sarodnick F, Brau H. Methoden der Usability Evaluation: wissenschaftliche Grundlagen und praktische Anwendung. Bern: Huber; 2006. p. 251

[22] Sutcliffe A, Gault B. Heuristic evaluation of virtual reality applications. Interacting with Computers. 2004;**16**(4):831-849

[23] Rusu C, Munoz R, Roncagliolo S, Rudloff S, Rusu V, Figueroa A. Usability heuristics for virtual worlds. In: AFIN International Conference on Advances in Future Internet. France: Nice/Saint Laurent du Var; 2011

[24] Murtza R, Monroe S, Youmans RJ. Heuristic evaluation for virtual reality systems. Proceedings of the Human Factors and Ergonomics Society Annual Meeting. 2017;**61**(1):2067-2071

[25] Gale N, Mirza-Babaei P, Pedersen I. Heuristic Guidelines for Playful Wearable Augmented Reality Applications. In: Proceedings of the 2015 Annual Symposium on Computer-Human Interaction in Play. London United Kingdom: ACM; 2015. pp. 529-534

[26] Endsley TC, Sprehn KA, Brill RM, Ryan KJ, Vincent EC, Martin JM. Augmented reality design heuristics: Designing for dynamic interactions. Proceedings of the Human Factors and Ergonomics Society Annual Meeting. 2017;**61**(1):2100-2104

[27] Bolder A, Grünvogel SM, Angelescu E. Comparison of the usability of a car infotainment system in a mixed reality environment and in a real car. In: Proceedings of the 24th ACM Symposium on Virtual Reality Software and Technology. Tokyo Japan: ACM; 2018. pp. 1-10

[28] Cavalcanti VC, de Santana MI, Gama AEFD, Correia WFM. Usability assessments for augmented reality motor rehabilitation solutions: A systematic review. International Journal of Computer Games Technology. 2018;**2018**:1-18

[29] Geisen E, Bergstrom JR. Usability Testing for Survey Research. Cambridge, MA: Morgan Kaufmann Publisher; 2017

[30] Kalawsky RS. VRUSE—A computerised diagnostic tool: For usability evaluation of virtual/synthetic environment systems. Applied Ergonomics. 1999;**30**(1):11-25

[31] Barnum CM. Usability Testing and Research. New York, N.Y: Longman; 2002

[32] Pabst M. General Data Protection Regulation (GDPR) – Official Legal Text [Internet]. General Data Protection Regulation (GDPR). 2022. Available from: https://gdpr-info.eu/

[33] Unternehmensberatung A. Datenschutz-Grundverordnung (DSGVO) - JUSLINE Österreich [Internet]. 2022. Available from: https://www.jusline.at/gesetz/dsgvo

[34] What is Samsung Gear 360 camera?. Samsung uk. 2022. Available from: https://www.samsung.com/uk/support/mobile-devices/what-is-samsung-gear-360-camera/

[35] MAX 6K Waterproof 360-Degree Action Camera | GoPro. 2022. Available from: https://gopro.com/en/us/shop/cameras/max/CHDHZ-202-master.html

[36] 360-degree camera RICOH THETA. 2022. Available from: https://theta360.com/en/

[37] RICOH THETA Z1. 2022. Available from: https://theta360.com/de/about/theta/z1.html

[38] Oculus Quest 2. Oculus Quest 2: Unser bisher bestes, neues all-in-one VR-Headset | Oculus [Internet]. Oculus Quest 2. 2022. Available from: https://www.oculus.com/quest-2/?locale=de_DE

[39] Blog MD. How-to: Spectator View, a new tool to help others see what you see in HoloLens [Internet]. Microsoft Devices Blog. 2017 2022. Available from: https://blogs.windows.com/devices/2017/02/13/spectator-view-new-tool-help-others-see-see-hololens/